HOCKEY'S HOME

HALIFAX-DARTMOUTH

THE ORIGIN OF CANADA'S GAME

MARTIN JONES

NIMBUS
PUBLISHING LTD

Nimbus Publishing Limited
PO Box 9166
Halifax, NS   B3K 5M8
(902) 455-4286

Printed and bound in Canada
Design: Arthur Carter

Cover Image: This Starr Manufacturing Company advertisement features a hockey player with his Starr skates and Mi'kmaq (MicMac) hockey stick. The identical image is painted on a large mural in Windsor, Nova Scotia, under the caption "Birthplace of Hockey" with one significant change: The star on the sweater (the logo for Dartmouth's Starr Manufacturing) has been replaced by a large "W." Many images from the Dartmouth Heritage Museum's Starr advertisement collection have been used throughout this book.

Author photo, back cover: Ann Jones

National Library of Canada Cataloguing in Publication Data

Jones, Martin W. (Martin William), 1960–
Hockey's Home: Halifax-Dartmouth: the origin of Canada's game/ Martin W. Jones.

Includes bibliographic references.
ISBN 1-55109-408-8

1. Hockey—Nova Scotia—Halifax—History. 2. Hockey—Nova Scotia—Dartmouth —History. I. Title.

GV848.4.C3J65 2002   796.962'09716'225   C2002-905054-5

Canadä   The Canada Council | Le Conseil des Arts
          for the Arts | du Canada

We acknowledge the financial support of the Government of Canada through the Book Publishing Industry Development Program (BPIDP) and the Canada Council for our publishing activities.

This book is dedicated to two
exceptional Nova Scotian historians,
Dr. John P. Martin and Dr. C. Bruce Fergusson,
and two exceptional people in my life,
my grandfather, Frank J. Martin,
and my brother, David Martin Jones.

ACKNOWLEDGEMENTS

I would like to acknowledge those who have assisted me with this book. Faith Wallace of the Dartmouth Heritage Museum, the staff of the Nova Scotia Archives and Records Management, and Stephen Coutts from the Nova Scotia Sport Hall of Fame have been a tremendous help. Thanks to publisher Dorothy Blythe of Nimbus for allowing me to share this history with you, Sandra McIntyre for her editorial assistance and support, and Arthur Carter for his design work. Norman Fergusson's phone call played an important role in my pursuing this topic and I would once again like to express my gratitude to him. Dr. John Martin's daughter, Sister Mary Martin, made this book possible by sharing with me over the last fifteen years copies of articles written by her late father. Many others directly or indirectly assisted with this book: Laurinda Desrochers, Heather Bryan, Takashi Osawa, Dr. Henry Bishop of the Black Cultural Centre, John MacLeod, Paul Barry, Shirley Barber, Gerald Martin, Tom Forrestall, Frank Garner, Peter Stickings, Barry Smith, Debbie O'Brien, Philip Hartling, Mitch Dickey, Alexa Thompson, Virginia Clark, Milly Riley, Tom Caldwell, Ian Scott, Daniel Brownlow, Carmen Moir, Bill Fitsell, Bruce Bowser, Paul and Vickie Williams, David and Diane Krochko. And finally, a special thanks to my parents, David and Marie Jones, my mother-in-law, Anna Ruth Rogers, and my family, Ann, David and Catherine, for their input and support.

TABLE OF CONTENTS

PREFACE

"Hockey is Canada's national game and
its greatest contribution to world sport."
—*The Canadian Encyclopedia* (2000)

Although it is generally accepted that the game of hockey originated in Canada, there is no consensus as to which town or city within our great country deserves to claim hockey as its own. This lack of agreement is due in part to the fact that hockey was not born or discovered, but, rather, evolved out of a complex set of conditions—environmental, social, and commercial—sometime in the late eighteenth or early nineteenth century. Nowhere were these conditions more fully realized, nowhere did so many elements necessary to the formation of the game come together, than in Halifax/Dartmouth, Nova Scotia. For this reason, Halifax/Dartmouth deserves to be called "hockey's home."

In this book, I discuss several of the significant historical events that contributed to the development of the game in these sister cities—now part of a larger municipality known as Halifax Regional Municipality—as well as information on related topics, such as skating. Because hockey is also part of my family history, this book is also, by necessity, personal. My grandfather, Frank J. Martin, was the first to suggest to me that hockey originated in Dartmouth. My grandfather's brother, Dr. John Martin, penned a history of Dartmouth in 1957 that has proven invaluable both for the references it makes to hockey and its history of the area in general. (I recently assisted Dr. Martin's daughter, Sister Mary Martin, and his son, John (Bud), in having this important book deposited with the National Library in Ottawa.) From these familiar sources, I set out to research hockey's early history more fully, spending countless hours in the public archives of Nova Scotia and the Dartmouth Heritage Museum, like my great-uncle before me. At every turn, I found more evidence—newspaper articles, diary entries, images—pointing to Halifax/Dartmouth as the place where this unique game was transformed into our country's favourite sport.

Armed with this information, in January 2002, I contacted the Halifax *Mail-Star* to reveal my findings and suggest that further research into hockey's origins was needed. After an article on the topic appeared in *The Mail-Star*, I received what turned out to be a very important phone call from Mr. Norman Fergusson, who directed me to the work of his late brother, Dr. Bruce Fergusson. The Rhodes

Scholar, provincial archivist, and Dalhousie professor had researched the birth-place of hockey issue in the 1960s and published a paper on the topic. Soon after, I discovered an article written by Dr. Martin in 1955 entitled "The Birthplace of Hockey." The work of these well-respected and highly qualified historians convinced me further that hockey originated in Halifax/Dartmouth, and I felt obliged to continue the search they had started.

In tracing this history and the development of our national game, I have consulted numerous contemporary sources, mostly newspapers, as well as books and articles on the subject. In a debate sometimes marred by misinformation and a lack of proper documentation, I have been especially careful to provide source information for all reference material I consulted in the course of my research. Endnotes provide the origin of all information cited. I hope the evidence I have unearthed will convince you, as it has me, that Halifax/Dartmouth truly is hockey's home.

THE ORIGIN OF HOCKEY IN HALIFAX/DARTMOUTH: A TIMELINE

While Windsor, Nova Scotia, relies on a fictional description of hurley published in 1844 as the basis for its birthplace of hockey claim, and Montreal points to a game imported by Halifax's J.G.A. Creighton in 1875, Halifax/Dartmouth offers an extensive array of evidence to support its claim as hockey's home.

1700s

Mi'kmaw history indicates that the Mi'kmaq played a game on ice on Tuft's Cove, Dartmouth, with eight men on each team and a wooden puck.

1827

Poem appears in Halifax's *Acadian Magazine*: "Now at ricket with hurlies* some dozens of boys/Chase the ball o'er ice, with a deafening noise."
*Ricket: a term for hockey. Hurley: a hockey stick.

1831

Townsfolk and the military enjoy a spirit-stirring game of wicket (hockey) on the North West Arm. Silhouette artist Hankes of Halifax cuts portrait of young Henry Piers holding a hockey stick.

1842

Local newspaper reports the Dartmouth Lakes as "good for a game of ricket [hockey]...a great match today, if the weather be fine."

1840s

A Mrs. Gould of Dartmouth describes the sport of hockey, popular during her childhood, circa 1840: "The Dartmouth Lakes and the small ponds were the only resorts of skaters and ricket players—the game now known as hockey...William Foster...always stood ricket guard [goaltender] with his creepers on, as he was not a skater."

1853

Local newpapers report the North West Arm "covered with skaters with their hurlies [hockey sticks]."

1859

On Dartmouth's lakes, young men play rickets [hockey] with "skates strapped on, and hurly in hand."

1860s

Starr Manufacturing Company advertisements for Starr skates and Rex and Mic-Mac hockey sticks appear.

1863

First hockey game played indoors at Halifax's first indoor rink. Poem proclaims: "Off we shoot, and poise and wheel: And swiftly turn upon scoring heel." John Forbes' spring skates first made at Dartmouth's Starr Manufacturing Company.

1864

Halifax/Dartmouth newspaper reports "boys...are playing hockey on the ice...upon skates" and debates the pros and cons of the sport, with some decrying "hockey not only annoying but dangerous."

1866

Starr Manufacturing patents the Forbes Acme Skate—the first modern skate. "The greatest skate factory in the world" sells over eleven million skates worldwide from 1863 to 1939.

1867

The *Halifax Reporter* writes that the centre of Dartmouth's Oathill Lake was occupied by "officers of the Garrison and the Fleet in a match game called hockey, i.e., ricket."

1875

On the North West Arm, a "boisterous and lively" game of rickets (hockey) is played till night fall. Halifax's J.G.A. Creighton suggests that Montreal friends take up the game of ice hockey, which they play using Halifax sticks and by "Halifax Rules."

"Here's a shot. Henderson made a wild stab for it and fell. Here's another shot, right in front. They score! Henderson has scored for Canada!"

—Foster Hewitt, game eight, Moscow, September 28, 1972

FOREWORD

I read *Hockey's Home* during the reunion of Canada's team of the century on the thirtieth anniversary of the 1972 Canada—Russia Super Series. The timing was perfect to reflect on our country's hockey heritage and the early roots of our national game.

Martin Jones has provided a compelling case that ice hockey originated in Dartmouth and Halifax. I especially enjoyed the descriptions of the early games on Lake Banook and the North West Arm, and was fascinated to learn of the development of the hockey stick and goals, the various rules of the game, and the tremendous contribution of the Starr Manufacturing Plant in the invention and production of the modern hockey skate. The first hockey games, the early hockey leagues and rinks, the first Black and female hockey teams—this book provides an almost endless array of hockey history.

The early references to the development of hockey on Dartmouth's lakes and Martin's own reminiscing of his love of the game bring back special memories of my youth playing hockey on the ponds of Lucknow, Ontario. Although scoring Team Canada's winning goal was the highlight of my professional career, I agree that nothing compares to playing pond hockey as a young boy with my friends on cold winter days.

Although I was disappointed to learn than Martin Jones is not a Leafs fan, there is no doubt that *Hockey's Home* is a great read that any hockey enthusiast will thoroughly enjoy. Congratulations Martin!

Paul Henderson
October, 2002

INTRODUCTION

HOCKEY'S HOME:
HALIFAX/DARTMOUTH

It was a beautiful day in early February. The sun was shining brightly in a cloudless sky, and the temperature was just above freezing with only a slight wind. Glassy Lake Banook was like a mirror, covered here and there with tiny patches of pure white wind-swept snow. My brother, David, and I were the two happiest boys in the city of Dartmouth: we had escaped from school with our mother's permission and were skating, hockey sticks in hand, on the most perfect day of the winter. David, the better skater, flew ahead of me in a flash, while I, the better stick-handler, wove in and out of imaginary N.H.L. defencemen and goaltenders. Only the periodic thunderous ring of expanding ice interrupted us. I was Jean Beliveau playing in the Stanley Cup final...I was...I was...flat on my face! My skate caught on a large crack in the ice and down I went.

After some consoling from my brother, we resumed our heavenly skate and were soon joined by numerous friends for a hotly contested game of hockey. The only disappointment of the afternoon was that someone permanently borrowed my new and fashionable Greb Kodiak work boots, and I had to walk home on my skates.

I can't remember when I first became a hockey fan. The fact that my mother, Marie, went skating before heading to the hospital for my birth might have had something to do with it. I grew up next to Sullivan's Pond, just below Lake Banook, in downtown Dartmouth. Until the flow of the water was changed to accommodate flood-proofing for the city's downtown after Hurricane Beth in 1971, Sullivan's Pond was our preferred hockey venue, especially since we could walk home for lunch, dinner, or hot chocolate with our skates on. Unfortunately, around the same time, the city stopped clearing and lighting the pond and the lake for skating—though this did little to stop us from using the pond at night. My parents had to convince me to join organized hockey at age eight or nine, and although I enjoyed many years of league hockey, with great players and coaches, nothing compared to playing with my friends on one of Dartmouth's many lakes. Like so many National Hockey League players who reminisce about their favourite hockey experiences on lakes, ponds, or rivers in their youth, my enjoyment of pond hockey, as we used to call it, was unbeatable.

My grandfather, Frank Martin, and his brothers, William (known as Dee) and John, began skating on Lake Banook in the 1890s, and their love of skating and hockey lasted throughout their lives. An avid hockey fan and one of the organizers of Dartmouth's first hockey league, Uncle Dee would watch *Hockey Night in Canada* with us in the late 1960s and aggravate my father, brother, and me with his periodic pronouncements on the state of Canadian hockey: "They aren't as good as the Russians!" he would exclaim. My brother and I attributed this opinion to the drink of rum that Dad always gave Dee to sip during the game. But when the Russians showed us just how good they were in the Super Series of 1972, Uncle Dee looked on with a knowing twinkle in his eye while we, like most Canadians, watched in shock.

In his later years, Uncle Dee switched from hockey to figure skating, and was well-known in the community as a skating instructor. Among his students were Evelyn McCall, who joined the Ice Capades in 1956, and her son, Robert McCall, Dartmouth's Olympic silver medalist. After Uncle Dee's death in 1981, Mrs. McCall wrote, "One man I knew would skate just for fun—Uncle Dee, the old smoothie. I'll never forget him as long as there is ice."[1] She also referred to a tradition that I had almost forgotten about, one Uncle Dee and my grandfather always practised when heading to the lakes for a skate: they brought along a baked potato to keep their boots warm and for a quick snack after some hours in the cold. Dee, who

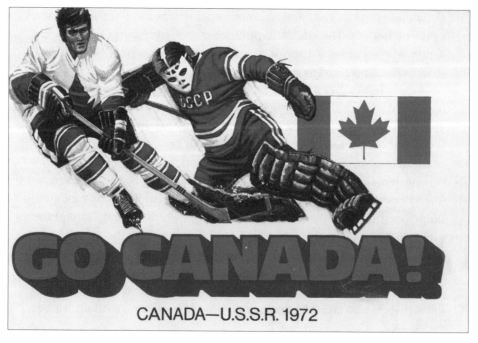

CANADA—U.S.S.R. 1972

My brother, David, and I (centre) with two friends playing hockey on Sullivan's Pond.

Below: My father and brother face-off on Sullivan's Pond with my grandfather, Frank Martin, age eighty.

St. Peter's Hockey Team, Champions of Dartmouth Amateur League, 1914, from left to right: (front row) R. Linterman (centre), R. Smith (utility wing); G. De Louchry (goal), F. Martin, captain (centre point), G. O'Hearn (right wing), C. Griffin (utility point); (back) J. Smith (left wing), W.P. Behan (manager).

Brothers Frank and Dee Martin, both in their eighties, enjoy hockey on our backyard rink in the 1960s.

continued to skate well into his eighties, was honoured by the town of Dartmouth in 1971 for "teaching the fine art of waltzing on skates to literally thousands of young people."[2]

Growing up and living in Dartmouth, I developed a keen interest in our history, influenced in no small part by my grandfather and my great-uncle John, author of *The Story of Dartmouth*. Born in 1886, John Martin was a high school teacher and vice-principal whose passion was always local history. In the 1930s, John and his brother James T. Martin, a well-known marathon runner, began writing articles on local history for the *Dartmouth Patriot* newspaper; from these articles grew *The Story of Dartmouth*, a chronicle of the town's history from 1750 until the 1940s. The preface to this interesting book reveals the high scholarly standards to which Dr. Martin held himself:

> In compiling the story, I sought out original sources where-ever possible, making a systematic study of the earliest Crown Land grants and the first hundred years of property transfers, thumbing through reams of manuscripts and old newspapers, besides visiting and telephoning repeatedly every elderly resident.

In his later years, Dee Martin switched from hockey to figure skating and taught thousands of Dartmouthians to skate. In this 1953 photo by Gene Mattatal, Dee is shown with Ruth Brown and Marie O'Toole at a skating carnival. Halifax's J.G.A. Creighton, who exported the Halifax hockey rules to Montreal in the 1870s, had a similar interest in figure skating, having been a skating judge in both cities.

DR. JOHN MARTIN
1886-1969

Dartmouth historian John Martin has arguably done more than anyone in the history of the city to record its rich and extensive history. In addition to his major history on the area, *The Story of Dartmouth*, Dr. Martin wrote numerous articles and pamphlets of importance, including "The Babes in the Woods," "The Birthplace of Hockey," and "Hockey in the Old Days." According to my research, Dr. Martin was the first historian to note Judge Haliburton's fictional reference to hurley in Windsor.[3]

Before becoming a school teacher, Dr. John Martin worked at the Western Union telegraph office in Halifax. He was working in this office when the first telegraph reports of the sinking of the *Titanic* arrived in Halifax. A few years later, Dr. Martin was teaching at St. Patrick's School on Barrington Street. He moved from the front of the class to discipline a student just as the Halifax Explosion hit, forcing the front wall of the classroom to collapse. He would later introduce the student as the man who saved his life.

More than thirty years after his death, I am certain that "Uncle John" would be extremely disappointed to learn that Dartmouth, one of the oldest settlements in Canada, can claim only one provincially designated historic building and not one national historic site.

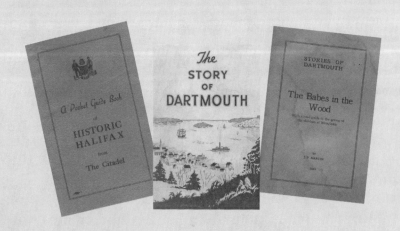

This self-imposed task occupied most of my spare time over a period of five years. It has carried me and my note-book to the New York Public Library, twice the Dominion Archives at Ottawa, countless days and nights in the Nova Scotia Archives, the Legislative Library, the Registry of Deeds, of Probate, of Crown Lands, the Dartmouth Ferry records, the Town hall records, church registers, school registers, besides extensive research among the private papers of old families, and among headstones in graveyards. (At Geary Street cemetery the Dunn family took me inside their antique vault to gaze upon one of the adult skeletons.)

In addition to the mass of manuscripts at the Nova Scotia Archives, I combed all the available issues of at least one Halifax or Dartmouth newspaper in every year from 1752 to 1920; often getting nothing of interest, and at other times turning up a mine of information. This was also my experience at the office of the Registry of Deeds where I searched through the first 85 books, and scanned some 40,000 pages, pausing when necessary to note down descriptions of plans of Dartmouth properties.

At various stages of the work, all this material was sifted, sorted, put into proper sequence, and after a sufficient amount of copy was typed to fill 32 book-pages, it went to the linotype operator. My next job was to read galley proofs, put in corrections, then transport the type homeward to make up the pages. Again back to the print shop with the precious pages occasionally getting piled in the trunk of a car, and finally rendering assistance of the pressman while he rolled off the required 1,000 copies. This printing routine was repeated about every three months.[4]

My father, David, recalls that Dr. Martin was locked in the Registry of Deeds vault one Friday evening after failing to hear the warning that the vault was being closed—no doubt because he was engrossed in some new piece of history. He poked around in the dark vault for a few hours before finding a phone to call for his rescue. Evidence of Dr. Martin's enthusiasm for his research is not gone forever: his hand-written notes appear in the margins of many old Halifax and Dartmouth papers held in local archives.

Granddad shared with me his memories about the Halifax Explosion, Haley's Comet, the Depression, and life during the war years. Our mutual love of hockey often led us to discussions about the early years of the game, including the rover, sideways nets, and lignum vitae pucks, which were made from a very hard Jamaican wood. Granddad told me the story of one game where the puck split and an argument ensued as to whether a half goal should be posted for the piece that broke off and went into the net! What stood out in my mind most, however, was his claim that ice hockey originated on Lake Banook in Dartmouth.

Granddad was not alone in this belief: Halifax/Dartmouth has been a player in a debate about hockey's origins that has been ongoing in Canada for more than seventy-five years. As the setting for countless games of hockey on lakes, ponds, and indoor rinks throughout the nineteenth century and perhaps earlier (with games documented in the newspaper as early as 1831)[5]; as the place where much of the equipment—skates, sticks, and nets—for the newly evolved game was first developed and manufactured; as the hometown of James George Aylwin Creighton, the man who introduced the game and the "Halifax Rules" to Montreal in 1875; and as the undisputed originator of a number of key elements of the game still in use today, including goaltenders and the forward pass, Halifax/Dartmouth can make a powerful case for the primacy of its hockey heritage.

Windsor (Nova Scotia), Montreal, and Kingston have all laid claim to the honour of being recognized as the birthplace of the sport, giving rise to a healthy debate on the issue. In a country where playing hockey is almost synonymous with being Canadian, the stakes are high, and consensus has been hard to come by, in part because hockey developed gradually, with early games rarely documented in detail, but also because agreement about what the birthplace claim entails and what kind of evidence should be considered has been lacking. Windsor cites a line in a fictional work written by Thomas Chandler Haliburton in 1844 as proof of its parentage, while Montreal uses a well-documented hockey game at Victoria Skating Rink in 1875 as the basis for its claim. Kingston has argued that a game played between the Royal Military College and Queen's University in 1886 and the formation of a hockey league shortly thereafter made it hockey's rightful birthplace, although it is now generally agreed that hockey could not have started in Kingston.[6] From early newspaper reports and other written accounts about hockey to the essential equipment developed by Starr Manufacturing, a wide range of evidence exists to support Halifax/Dartmouth's case.

The publication in June 2002 of an eighteen-page report looking into the Windsor claim has fuelled the intensity of the debate. Released by the Society for International Hockey Research (SIHR), a self-appointed group whose objective it is "to establish an accurate historical account of the game of hockey," the report finds that "the Windsor proponents do not meet the test of documenting the first game of hockey played in Windsor, Nova Scotia."[7] Although they have yet to name the city they will endorse officially, the SIHR appears to favour Montreal, citing the March 3, 1875, game at the Victoria Skating Rink at Stanley and Drummond streets as "...unique. It is the earliest eyewitness account known, at least to this SIHR committee, of a specific game of hockey in a specific place at a specific time, and with a recorded score, between two identified teams."[8] In a report purportedly about Windsor, the attention it gives to Montreal is surprising, especially when Kingston elicits only a cursory response and Halifax/Dartmouth almost none at all. SIHR support for the Montreal claim based on this evidence is even more surprising given the committee's move to broaden the definition of hockey and thereby avoid the need for such "specific" documentation. The new definition encompasses "rudimentary forms of the game as well as present features" by defining hockey as a game played on an ice surface "in which two opposing teams of skaters, using curved sticks, try to drive a small disc, ball or block into or through the opposite goals."[9] With some of the Halifax/Dartmouth material in hand—material that both meets the requirements of this definition of hockey and pre-dates the 1875 game in Montreal—the SIHR committee continued the recent trend toward ignoring Halifax and Dartmouth's significant hockey heritage. Clarifying the term "hockey" and including in the definition only the fundamental elements of the game benefits the debate as a whole, but such benefits cannot be gained if they are not properly applied to all of the available evidence.

The connection between Montreal's hosting of the 1875 game and its status as the birthplace of hockey is weak—it is never made clear how the Montreal game might lead to the conclusion that Montreal is the birthplace of our beloved national sport. Given the significant part Halifax/Dartmouth played in making that 1875 game in Montreal happen, this conclusion is not logical. It was, after all, Halifax native James G. Creighton who introduced hockey to Montreal in 1875, and it was using Halifax/Dartmouth hockey sticks and by "Halifax Rules" that the game was played. Before Montrealers could have their "organized game," enthusiasts in Halifax and Dartmouth had been playing hockey—a game between two teams on ice with skates and sticks, the objective of which was to put an object between the opposite goal posts—for forty years or more, including organized games on indoor rinks. But really, these "firsts" are not the mainstay of Halifax/Dartmouth's relationship to early hockey in Canada. In the end, the "hockey's home" birthright belongs to Halifax/Dartmouth because of the overwhelming influence it had on the initial development of the game and the pivotal role it played in guaranteeing hockey's continued evolution. As the evidence now stands, no other place can say the same.

In the face of such compelling evidence, it has been suggested that the game of hockey in Halifax and Dartmouth was played on a sporadic basis in its formative years, both outdoors and indoors.[10] However, in many of the newspapers from the 1800s, the game of hockey received little coverage not because it wasn't popular but because it was a regular, everyday winter occurrence. Plus, most newspapers were not published on a daily basis and they usually consisted of only three to five pages. Much of the space was occupied by advertisements, editorials, letters to the editor and news events such as the American Civil War, the exploration of the Amazon River, and Canadian Confederation. There was no "sports section," and reports of sporting events were infrequent. Most references to hockey were to inform the public of excellent skating conditions or unusual events at the lakes such as a near-drowning or the appearance of a military band.

In *The Halifax Reporter* of February 19, 1867, sports played an unusually prominent role. Alongside advertisements and news about local politics, the possible impeachment of American president Andrew Johnson, and the upcoming

Paris Exhibition, a "grand curling match" on the Dartmouth Lakes was men-tioned—significant, no doubt, because a gold medal was to be awarded at the match. The North West Arm was said to be in tolerable condition, and a garrison and fleet "hockey match" and another upcoming game were noted—the ice up-date being the key item. In the same issue of *The Halifax Reporter*, a hockey game on Oathill Lake in Dartmouth was reported, with the new location, the fashions of the day, the music provided by the band, and the "forebodings of a conflict" as the focus of the article:

Skating Scribblings by Icicle

The North West Arm being rough, Maynard's Lake bleak and partly open, the 1st and 2nd Dartmouth decidedly sheety, skaters cast about for good ice, and by some unknown means the initiated were informed of there being a good surface on the almost unknown 'Oathill Lake,' where our grandfathers fished fifty years ago. There are several ways of getting to this pretty little "sheet," but the most direct route is to cross Maynard's lake diagonally form the pipe-house in a northerly direction, this brings us to a rugged pathway up a steep hill , and after a long descent 'Oathill' bursts upon the view. On Saturday the lake was covered with skaters of both sexes, there being about 1500 there during the afternoon. In every direction pretty sylphlike forms were to be seen either cutting the 'outside edge' independently, or timidly learning to 'stroke out', aided by the strong arms of the sterner sex. Some of the ladies' costumes were charming: jaunty fur caps, tight-fitting jackets and looped up skirts, showing the bright-colored petticoats and hose: neat boots, and in most cases the Acme Skate.[11] Rosy cheeks predominated, and many pale ones were flushed with a returning tinge of health, brought by the fresh air and pleasant excitement of the scene. The deep green forest shuts in the lake and makes a deep green fringe to a very pretty scene.

Two well contested games of 'ricket' were being played. At the upper end were a number of young men from Dartmouth and the City, playing their 'hurleys' and 'following up' the ball, while the cen-tre was occupied by a number of officers of the Garrison and Fleet, in a match game called hockey i.e. ricket. The boundary lines of each game were not well defined and occasionally the 'aristocratic hock-ey ball' would encroach on the upper game, when the 'plebeian hur-leys' would pass it around for a time and send it back again to the select circle. Very little science was displayed in either game, the old class of players seem to have died out, and their successors are not up in the science of leading off the ball, doubling and carrying it

through. Instead of the old style, the game as now played is dangerous to outsiders, especially to ladies, some of whom were rather
roughly treated in the scrimmages after the ball. There was not ten-
derness displayed in the 'United Service Game', as many sore shins
can testify, and more than one poor little middy got a stretcher from
their heavier antagonists of the land service. Some small boys had
the hardihood and impudence to raise their hurleys to strike the
'swell ball' as it passed them, for which flagrant crime they were visited with condign punishment. This was not relished by the friends
of the juveniles, who after their own fashion encroached upon and
took partial possession of the select territory which, during infringement resulted in terrible forebodings of a conflict between
both sides, but although a forest of sticks and hurleys were raised in
the air, not a head was broke, or, as Pat said at Donnybrook, 'six o'-
clock came and no blow struck.' However, the 'exclusives' had to
abandon their game and retire from the field with their 'hot porter'
apparatus,[12] which had been well patronized during the day. To the

*Being a major military base and naval port, Halifax was home to numerous soldiers, and
sailors who played an important hockey role both on and off the ice. While many played the
game and helped it spread to other areas of Canada, others provided musical entertainment
at the lakes as noted in many newspaper reports from the 1800s. In this photograph, the
Princess Louise Fusileers are on parade in the Governor's Field, circa 1885.*

bystanders it was great fun, and it would be hard to say which side behaved the best or the worst. This much must be said, that if exclusive games of hockey are to be played, a crowded lake is no place for it, and as it is the established custom for every one who chooses to take a hand in it is next to impossible to play match games except on unfrequented ice. Some fishermen cut fishing holes through the ice in eager search for the little trout that are said to be in abundance, thus making ugly holes in which to get a cold bath. The evenings now are very beautiful; and six o'clock comes too early, but a knowledge of a not too well defined path through the woods being between us and the road hurries one off before the shades of evening close, so reluctantly we quit the really beautiful lake for the smoky atmosphere of the city.

Yesterday Oathill was enlivened by the strains of music, the 4th band being posted in the woods near the north end of the lake, adding materially to the enjoyment of the large number present. The ice is not as good as it was on Saturday, but is daily improving.

Hockey evolved out of a complex set of conditions and influences that, like other evolutionary processes, determined its final shape and character. There is no question that Windsor, Montreal, Kingston, and other Canadian locales have all contributed in their way to the game we play today. But in Halifax and Dartmouth, the right combination of people and conditions came together to create the setting from which hockey first emerged. It was in Halifax and Dartmouth that a game on ice using skates and hockey sticks first adopted the markers of hockey proper. Finally, from the first organized indoor games to the development of hockey equipment at the Starr Manufacturing Company, Halifax and Dartmouth ensured that the game could continue to evolve as it was played by more and more Canadians across the country.

PART I

THE PERFECT CONDITIONS

Two hundred and fifty years ago in Halifax/Dartmouth, a number of forces came together to create conditions ideal for the evolution of hockey. The natural landscape, with its numerous lakes and large natural harbour, had for thousands of years attracted the native Mi'kmaq to the area. In winter the Mi'kmaq played a game on the ice with wooden sticks and a stone, and mastered the skill of stick-carving. The establishment of a military fortress at Halifax brought thousands of healthy and exuberant soldiers and sailors to the new capital. With the growth of the settlement came plans for economic development, the major project being the construction of the Shubenacadie Canal along the unique waterway that stretches inland across the province. Dartmouth's population increased dramatically with the arrival of Irish and Scottish labourers to work on the canal. Just as the new settlers had to adapt to their new environment, the sporting traditions they brought with them had to be adapted as well—to the long, cold winters in particular. With abundant ice forming on the ponds, lakes, and even the harbour, outdoor winter recreation like skating and hockey became popular, and the creation of reliable ferry and omnibus services made it easy for local residents to get to their favourite outdoor recreation spots.

Created some two hundred million years ago, the Isthmus of Chignecto is Nova Scotia's only connection to mainland North America. Starting seventy-five thousand years ago, the last ice age retreated over its lands to create numerous lakes, over fifteen hundred large lakes in total, representing an area as big as Rhode Island.[1] The sister towns of Halifax and Dartmouth, settled by Europeans in 1749 and 1750 respectively, were also influenced by the ice's retreat. Separated by the second largest natural harbour in the world, Dartmouth would be blessed with twenty-three lakes and Halifax with a landscape that would make it an appropriate site for a military fortress. In 1749, Governor Edward Cornwallis wrote to His Majesty in England:

> Your Grace will see that the place I have fixed for the town is on the west side of the harbour, upon the side of a hill which commands the whole peninsula and shelters the town from the northwest winds. From the shore to the top of the hill is about half a mile. The slope is very gentle, the soil is good, there is convenient landing for boats all along the beach, and good anchorage within gunshot of the shore for the largest ships.[2]

View of Halifax, Nova Scotia from the Red Mill, Dartmouth, c. 1853

The following year, the *Alderney*, a small, three-masted barque, arrived in Halifax Harbour carrying over 350 passengers to their new home of Dartmouth. In his book *In the Wake of the Alderney*, Dartmouth author Harry Chapman writes:

> A number of locations were considered for the new settlement, but Cornwallis finally decided on the eastern side of the harbour near the big cove where the sawmill was located. Work began almost

immediately to hack away the forest in order to lay out a town plot and build homes for the new settlers before the onslaught of winter. The early settlement was made up of 11 rectangular blocks approximately 400 feet long and 200 feet wide. Each building lot measured 100 feet in length and 50 feet in width. The northern boundary of the settlement was present-day North Street, the western boundary the harbourfront, the southern boundary Dartmouth Cove and the eastern boundary present-day Victoria Road. The location of the new settlement had been for many years the summer encampment for the Mi'kmaq, which they referred to as Boonamoogwaddy—tomcod ground.[3]

The native Mi'kmaq had resided on the shores of the harbour and on Dartmouth's lakes for at least ten thousand years. They led a nomadic life, hunting, fishing, and gathering food. Mi'kmaw summer camps were located on the shores of Dartmouth from Eastern Passage to the head of Bedford Basin. "On this side of the harbour," writes Dr. John Martin, "geographical conditions were far more favourable for congregating, with three voluminous streams of never-failing fresh water flowing down to the estuaries of the two little bays, both later known as Mill Cove."[4] With the approach of winter, the tribes moved inland to hunt and fish

Chief Louis Paul is seated at left in this circa-1900 photograph of the Mi'kmaw encampment at Tufts Cove. The encampment was destroyed by the Halifax Explosion in 1917, at which time the surviving Mi'kmaq moved to the Shubenacadie area.

on the numerous lakes and rivers. The hills near the various bays of lakes Banook and MicMac afforded shelter from winds and furnished streams of fresh water; they were, therefore, the most favourable camp sites. Their presence would have a significant impact on the development of ice hockey.

THE SHUBENACADIE CANAL

The traditional Mi'kmaw water route, which was navigated in birchbark canoes, extended from Halifax Harbour through the Dartmouth Lakes and beyond to the Shubenacadie River and the Minas Basin. Where the waterways were not connected, the Mi'kmaq portaged. In England and North America during the late 1700s and early 1800s, "canal mania" had spread. By 1810, almost thirteen hundred miles of waterways had been built in Britain. Between 1817 and 1825, the Erie Canal system was constructed in Upper New York State, making New York City the busiest seaport on the east coast. The early settlers of Halifax and Dartmouth recognized the potential economic benefits of constructing a canal along the traditional Mi'kmaw route. Such a canal would enhance trade between the two regions and open up the interior of the province.[5]

In 1797, Nova Scotia's Legislative Assembly approved funding for a survey across the province from the harbour. The report suggested that twenty locks would be required to allow vessels to sail all the way to the Minas Basin from Dartmouth. Although a company was created to oversee the project, last-minute restrictions on the proposal caused the project to be put on hold.

Pressure on the government to promote a canal continued. In 1824, another feasibility study was concluded. Francis Hall, an engineer with canal-building experience, recommended in his report that five locks be used between the harbour and Lake Banook, with additional locks to connect the various lakes and waterways farther along the route. Almost one half of the cost of the entire project related to the first section from Halifax Harbour to Banook Lake.[6]

In 1826, the Shubenacadie Canal Company was incorporated, bringing the biggest economic boom to Dartmouth in over forty years. The commencement of construction was a major event in the new colony. On July 25, 1826, the first sod for the canal was turned by Lord Dalhousie, governor-general of British North

The Shubenacadie Canal played an important role in the history of Dartmouth. Many Scottish and Irish canal workers came to Dartmouth to live and work on the canal. In 1984, the Canadian Society for Civil Engineering named the Shubenacadie Canal a National Historic Civil Engineering Site.

America. Among the two thousand spectators were the lieutenant-governor, rear admiral, members of the government, and the principal officials of the canal company. Artillerymen boomed out a nineteen-gun salute and the band of the Rifle Brigade played "God Save the King." The Hon. Michael Wallace, the eighty-three-year-old master of ceremonies, proudly proclaimed:

> As I have been honored with the office of President, I cannot be a silent spectator of this first step of this important work. I have the confidence and pride to style myself the father of this project. It originated in my mind long before many of those who hear me, were born....I cannot expect to have many years added to my life, but it is not impossible that I may yet view the progress and even the completion of this great design....Our children, I venture to prophecy, will bless us for the undertaking, and our posterity will find it one of the best legacies bequeathed to them by their ancestors...[7]

Work on the canal proceeded, and in 1829 the last section, the Lake Banook connection to the harbour, including the holding area known as Sullivan's Pond, was commenced. But the section between the pond and the harbour required additional land purchases, an expense that began to tax the resources of the company, and by 1832, work on the project had ceased.

The workers that came to Dartmouth to construct the canal played an important role in our hockey history as many of them were employed at the Starr Manufacturing Plant and played the new game on Dartmouth's lakes.

Because of Dartmouth's small population, hundreds of skilled and unskilled workers were recruited from Scotland and Ireland to work on the canal. Stonecutters, masons, quarriers, carpenters, mechanics, and general labourers were sought after. In May, 1831, *Halifax Monthly Magazine* printed the following description of Dartmouth's new settlers:

> The increase in population which the Canal work produced in Dartmouth has occasioned a new settlement about a quarter of a mile from the water. This consists of about 40 huts and houses, raised for the greater part, by the laborers employed at the Canal; and called by some "Canal Town," and by others "Irish Town," because the majority of persons who own the little buildings are natives of Ireland. Irish Town affords a curious specimen of the first steps of civilization in a new country. The log houses and little enclosures are very rude, the stumps of the trees which form them stand all around, and in small openings in the brush, scraps of gardens appear.

The settlement also exhibits many primitive features of Irish rural life. On summer evenings, the groups reclining about the doors, show their proper quota of flaxen-haired chubby-cheeked youngsters, while from one or two taverns of the village, the scrapings of a fiddle, the squealings of a bagpipe and the shuffling of feet announce that the labors of the day were not sufficient to bow the everlasting mind, or to prevent zeal for the evening's exercise and pleasure.

The last houses of Irish Town are within about a stone's throw of the "Church with the steeple"; and the first houses of Dartmouth are within a stone's throw at the other side of the Church, so that a junction may be formed, and Irish Town becomes a suburb of its older neighbor.[8]

The construction of the canal would have a significant effect on the area. Not only did the arrival of canal workers from Ireland and Scotland boost the town's population; it provided both a skilled labour force for many of Dartmouth's future industries, including the Starr Manufacturing Company, and a group of young men eager to pursue the game of hockey in their new home. Naturally, these Irish and Scottish immigrants brought the games and sports of their home countries with them, which they played amongst themselves when their work was done:

A hurley match, a game at balls or bowls, throwing the sledge, leaping, or a jog, are commonly resorted to, as amusements after the work of the weekday, or the devotions of the Sabbath.[9]

In 1847, Charles Fairbanks, an engineer and builder of the Halifax water system, conducted his own survey of the canal and decided that the project had been conducted on an unnecessarily large scale. From the harbour to Lake Banook, he recommended the construction of shallow canal ways and an inclined plane instead of more locks, and the use of narrow boats.

In 1853, the Inland Navigation Company was incorporated and, in 1861, the canal was finally completed. The *Avery*, a sixty-ton side wheel steamer sixty-five

In 1861, the Inland Navigation Company's Avery *was the first vessel to successfully navigate the Shubenacadie Canal.*

HURLEY VS. HOCKEY

The various terms used to describe the game of hockey in the nineteenth century can be confusing. During the early 1800s, the Irish game of hurley or hurling, similar to the Canadian game of lacrosse, was played in Nova Scotia and other areas of the country. Although hurley was played infrequently toward the middle of the century, the new game of hockey was sometimes described as hurley.[10] Also, despite the significant difference between the hurley stick and the hockey stick, in the mid-1800s, the stick used in the game of hockey was often referred to as a hurley or hurly. To complicate matters, hockey was also frequently called wicket(s) or ricket(s), in reference to the goal posts, and in later years was sometimes called shinny. Fortunately, many newspaper accounts use these terms interchangeably, such as an article from 1867 which stated: "The centre of the lake was occupied by a number of officers of the Garrison and the Fleet in a match game called hockey, i.e. ricket."[11] As well, skating was a term used to include hockey—reports of good skating conditions were also intended to include hockey. As a result, the cover photo—a Starr ad featuring a hockey player—contained the caption: "Starr skates for star skaters."

This photograph of an old hurley stick and a hockey stick carved in Nova Scotia in 1865 shows the significant difference between the two. The hockey stick, carved from a single piece of wood, including the tree root, is much longer and was designed to propel the ball or puck on the ice surface. Hurley sticks are much shorter in length—on average 3 feet (91 cm.) long—and were designed to allow the player to catch the ball on the stick, run with it, and hurl it at the goal. The hurley goal posts are 16 feet high with a 21-foot-wide crossbar placed eight feet from the ground. Three points are awarded if the ball is hurled into the net strung between the posts; one point when the ball is hurled over the crossbar.[12]

feet long and fifteen feet wide, completed the first round trip from Dartmouth to Maitland on the Minas Basin. The canal operated for eight more years, moving products such as ice, sand, gravel, lime, gypsum and, ironically, railway ties, before being replaced by the railroad as the most economical and popular mode of transportation.[13] Although the canal was arguably a failure, its provision of a skilled workforce and a supply of water power for the Starr Manufacturing plant would have a significant influence on Canada's hockey history.

ICE FOR WORK AND PLAY

In the years following their founding, Halifax and Dartmouth were ideally suited to various kinds of outdoor activities, but those that helped the townsfolk pass the long winter months, like skating, sleighing, and sledding, were especially popular. With eight or ten thousand soldiers and sailors in a town with about as many permanent inhabitants, the harbour was busy with entertainment and sport in both the winter and summer months. The first regatta was held in Halifax Harbour in 1826 in honour of Lord Dalhousie's visit:

> All the warships in the harbour and numerous small craft were be-
> decked in colors for the occasion. The prize for first-class sailing
> boats was won by Admiral Lake, who steered the craft himself. The
> fishermen's races, however, pulling over the long course around
> George's Island, created much more interest. Besides the rowing
> contests, there was a canoe race open to native Indians. It was a new
> and novel sight for the crowds of spectators to see several canoes
> impelled with surprising velocity by Mic-Macs in their native cos-
> tume with their long black hair flying in the wind, and to hear their
> exciting shrieks of the most extraordinary yells as they dashed
> down the harbour. The regatta was such a decided success that it
> promised to become an annual affair. Money prizes were awarded
> the winners, chiefly in the canoe and rowing events.[14]

There was some concern, however, about the appropriateness of some of the activities that were taking place on Sundays. Joseph Howe, the Nova Scotian statesman who led the fight for responsible government in the British Commonwealth, followed this issue closely in his role as editor of *The Novascotian* in 1829. In *Joseph Howe Conservative Reformer 1804-1818*, J. Murray Beck explains that Howe preached "religious toleration" for those who, after working six days a week, wanted some "innocent recreation" on Sundays:

> In the same spirit, Howe protested against government restrictions
> that were unsuited to the age, especially when they had been hand-
> ed down from the hoary past. He became highly indignant when

SULLIVAN'S POND AND LAKE BANOOK

To celebrate the two-hundred-fiftieth anniversary of Dartmouth, the Halifax Foundation placed a marker at Sullivan's Pond, which reads:

> Sullivan's Pond was a vital feature of the historic Shubenacadie Canal, the traditional water route of Mi'kmaq Indians connecting the harbour at Dartmouth with Minas Basin and the Bay of Fundy. When the Canal operated, from 1861 to 1870, water from the Pond powered an incline railway which carried vessels along the quarter-mile route from the harbour to the Pond, the surface of which is more than 50 feet above mean harbour level. Irish stone-masons built a great circular dam in the 1830's, backing up the stream running from Lake Banook to the harbour and forming the Pond we enjoy today. The remains of the dam, now covered with earth, lie beneath your feet.

Adjacent to the Starr building, the inclined plane was used to carry boats by rail from Halifax Harbour to Sullivan's Pond. Two large wheels at each end of the rail turned a large cable that moved the iron-wheeled timber cradle up and down the inclined plane, carrying the canal boat. The cables were powered by either a vertical waterwheel or a water turbine.[15] A turbine using water from the canal was also used to power the Starr plant.

Sullivan and many of his fellow workmen lived in stone and log huts they built in "Irishtown," close to what is now Saint Peter's Church. The two stone pillars visible from here mark the channel running to the entrance to Lake Banook and the first lock of the Shubenacadie Canal.

Banook Canoe Club, circa 1920

Lake Banook has been a popular location for winter and summer sports for centuries. The site of the earliest hockey games in Nova Scotia, Lake Banook is also home to the Banook Canoe Club, which was incorporated in 1903 (making it one of the oldest canoe clubs in Canada). Many of the club's members played an important role in the development of ice hockey in the previous century, and in 1905, Banook entered a team in Dartmouth's first hockey league. In 1997, the World Canoe Championships were held at Lake Banook. Featuring over one thousand competitors from over forty-five countries, Canoe '97 was the largest international Olympic-sport championship ever held in Atlantic Canada.

H.W. Crawley was fined for skating on Sunday, even though he had attended church twice that same day, and expressed great satisfaction when, on appeal, the Supreme Court held that the Nova Scotian act, which was based on a British statute designed to cope with levity of manners during the reign on Charles I, could not be used to prohibit innocent recreation. Any other conclusion, he contended, would have been a direct breach of the religious toleration which we are supposed to enjoy.[16]

Early skates were often attached to the boot by boring a hole in the centre of the leather heel with a tool known as a gimlet. When the boots were not used for skating, the hole was plugged with a slim cylinder of paper.

This debate provoked many a remark in the local papers, and as the years progressed, it appears only to have intensified—perhaps as a result of the increased popularity of skating and hockey. In 1853, *The Acadian Recorder* solemnly reported:

> Last Sunday, the lake above Mr. Hostermans' was liberally covered with skaters, with their hurlies, and the small spots of ice available on the North West Arm were similarly occupied to the great pride of those upon it. We regret to add that many well-dressed females were to be seen in considerable numbers on the shores, enjoying the scene.[17]

The "scene," of course, refers to the hockey matches taking place at the best spots on the ice, with hockey sticks referred to as "hurlies," as was common at the time[18] ("skating" and "skaters," in fact, were often used to mean both ice skating or "fancy skating" and hockey). Hockey was apparently so familiar and so popular by this time that the women spectators "in considerable numbers" on a Sunday, and not the hockey games themselves, were of special note.

Recreation was not the only use Halifax/Dartmouth made of the abundant ice. A thriving ice industry was carried out in Dartmouth for over one hundred years, starting with William Foster building a small ice house near the Canal Bridge in 1836. In summer, the ice was transported by wheelbarrow to be sold at Foster's store near the ferry landing in Halifax. A thriving industry was soon in place. *The Halifax Reporter* declared in February 1867: "The Ice Companies and individual dealers are busy cutting and storing their crop which is to gladden the lovers of sherry cobblers and ice creams during the sultry days of summer."[19]

This illustration of the North West Arm from Canadian Illustrated *appeared on March 30, 1872, where it was noted: "The Arm, at Halifax…is the scene of frequent field days with the lovers of skating in the Acadian capital. On such occasions, the rank, beauty and fashion of the city turn out in hundreds, armed with the indispensable Acme Skate, for an afternoon's enjoyment of their winter pastime."*

Falling through the ice was always a risk when skating on the arm or one of many local lakes. In 1848, Chambers's Information for the People *contained this helpful information: "Skating on ice of doubtful strength is accompanied with great danger, as in an instant the skater may find himself sunk to the neck in water, and be drowned before assistance can be rendered. Much of this danger may be obviated by wearing a safety-cape, which is a loose cape, of some waterproof fabric, inflated with air. We recommend every skater to use by all means a cape of this kind while pursuing his amusement on the ice."*

Dr. Martin noted that the Dartmouth Lakes yielded an ice crop of exceptional quality compared to the poor quality of the New England crop in 1880. Firms including Glendenning, Chittick, Carter, Hutchinson, Lawlor, and Waddell stacked their ice-houses to the rafters and had to use vacant buildings near the harbour shore to house the overflow ice. An additional ice house was located at Maynard's Lake. Large sections of ice were sawed crosswise to a specified depth by a saw. Inside the building, short slides conveyed the blocks of ice to various levels, where gangs of workmen packed them in sawdust. During the summer and fall months, many schooners and square-rigged schooners, usually destined for large American ports, could be seen loading ice. The Dartmouth crop that year (1880) was twenty thousand tons with the price rising from $4 to $7 a ton in New York.[20]

The growth of the ice industry inevitably created a conflict with outdoor enthusiasts who were using the same lakes for recreational purposes. In fact, the unfortunate drowning of a skater on the Dartmouth Lakes prompted numerous letters to the editors of the local newspapers suggesting legislative intervention. The following letter to the editor was signed "PRECAUTION":

> It is with much concern that I have read "Humanity's" letter relative to the sad accident on the Dartmouth lake a few weeks ago, and urging that a bill be passed at this session of the legislature governing the cutting of ice on the lakes generally, and making it compulsory to place stakes around spots where the ice has been cut.

Dartmouth's ice industry was a key employer in the town for over a century. Although some hockey writers have suggested that our climate was not suitable for outdoor hockey, the ice industry clearly showed the extent of our winter season.

At present on the Dartmouth lakes, a few spruce bushes are all that mark these fatal spots. The recent sad drowning accident has led to much inquiry about the danger of skating in Dartmouth, and it is surprising to learn how very few understand the dread significance of these few spruce saplings fastened in the ice.

The lakes have been the favourite resort for skaters for many years and will continue so to be, but is it not our bounden duty to prevent loss of life by printed notices and proper safeguards?   I certainly agree with "Humanity" that it is indeed surprising that no inquest was held. I would respectfully suggest too that honourable body, the Dartmouth council, as well as to our own, that "Humanity's" letter be considered at the first opportunity.[21]

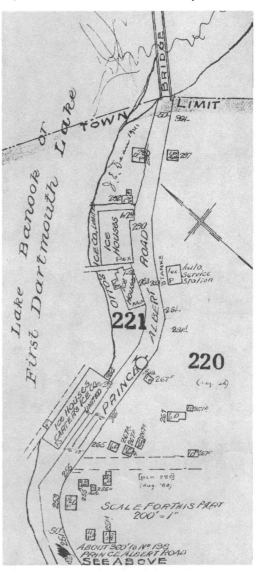

The winter climate created excellent conditions for ice on the harbour and the lakes of the area. In the winter of 1832, the weather continued cold with ice forming in the coves; by mid-February, temperatures were below -12 F (-24 C) and ice extended over the whole harbour. Hundreds of people amused themselves by skating across the harbour.[22] In late December 1844, a cold wave set in and by New Year's Day "skating on the lakes was enjoyed by a large crowd, many crossing from Halifax."[23] Another severe spell of weather arrived in 1847, and the newspapers reported that "there was superior skating on the Dartmouth Lakes."[24] In 1849,

This insurance plan from 1944 shows the location of some of the ice houses on Lake Banook, which provided ice for use during the summer months until the development of modern refrigerators.

"View on First Dartmouth Lake," c. 1855

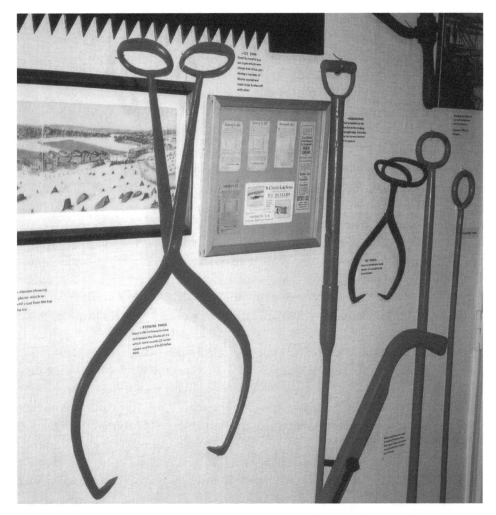

The Dartmouth Heritage Museum contains a significant collection of items of historical importance spanning the last 252 years. Included in the collection is an extensive display of items from the ice industry that operated on the town's lakes for over a century.

the harbour gradually froze until the ice extended to Mauger's Beech on McNab's Island. The upper part of the ice was usually the safest, and the popular landing place at Halifax was the soft beach near the foot of Cornwallis Street.[25] The heaviest snowfall in fifty-one years completely buried both towns on February 11 of 1849. In 1859, the harbour froze once again with a few days of skating in March and trotting races on Bedford Basin. In the winter of 1862, a four-ton boiler was moved over the ice on the Dartmouth Lakes to the Waverley gold mines.[26] In 1870, excellent ice conditions were once again reported:

One gathers from fragmentary sources that there were the usual outdoor activities that winter. A Halifax newspaper of January 22nd reported 12 inches of ice in Maynard's lake at Dartmouth, and "hundreds went over from Halifax on Saturday afternoon to enjoy the skating. The splendid band of the 78th Regiment went over also and discoursed sweet music at the lake. The wealth and beauty of Halifax were fully represented, and the scene was one of the rarest and most exhilarating description."[27]

Bedford Basin, the large body of water at the north end of the harbour, froze most winters, and its ice surface continued to be used by pedestrians and vehicles until the early 1930s.[28] My father, David, who grew up near the basin, played hockey on it until 1939, when the numerous convoys that assembled in its protected waters during World War Two prevented ice from forming the following winter. The suggestion that ice conditions in Halifax/Dartmouth in the nineteenth and well into the twentieth century were anything less than favourable for skating sports like hockey (the very argument put forward by the Canadian Amateur Hockey Association in 1943 in their attempt to substantiate the Kingston claim) is unfounded.[29]

Dartmouth's natural ice business on the Dartmouth Lakes collapsed after two unusually mild winters in 1950 and 1951. At the time, the ice business generated over $400,000 per year in business, and employed many men throughout the year, as many as two hundred more in the winter months.[30] Younger readers who take their family's refrigerator for granted will be surprised to learn from their parents or grandparents that weekly deliveries of ice were required to keep the home's ice box cool throughout the year. Many will recall receiving a cool treat from the ice wagon driver, or visiting the ice house in the summer to have a piece of ice chipped off a block buried in sawdust.

BETWEEN HALIFAX AND DARTMOUTH BY FERRY

When not iced over, the world's second largest natural harbour was a considerable barrier between the two new colonies, so a ferry service was started in 1752. John Connor was given an exclusive three-year contract to carry paying passengers from sunrise to sunset every day of the week, with an additional trip on Sunday for church services.[31] This ferry service has continued to the present day, making it the longest running salt-water ferry service in the world. Its unique history inspired a book, *Like A Weaver's Shuttle: A History of the Halifax-Dartmouth Ferries*, by Joan Payzant (my former grade four teacher) and her husband, Lewis.

As noted by the Payzants, the ferries had a significant impact on the ease with which "skatists" and "hockeyists" could get to the lakes when there was no ice on the harbour:

> The same ice which caused the ferries so much trouble and loss of revenue provided pleasure to hundreds of skaters. Many present-day residents of Halifax and Dartmouth recall hearing stories of their immediate forebears either skating or walking to work across the harbour. When the harbour itself was not ice covered (the normal state), the ferry company contributed to the whims of the skating enthusiasts. Haligonians as well as Dartmouthians enjoyed skating on the many lakes of Dartmouth. The minutes of the Steam Boat Company record that a flag was to be hoisted at the Halifax Station when there was good skating in Dartmouth.[32]

Although useful for skaters wishing to travel across the harbour to enjoy skating and games of hockey in either Dartmouth or Halifax, the ferries faced their own problems during the coldest periods of winter:

> January of 1898 was very cold and snowy, resulting in the worst harbor freeze-up since 1875. Mill Cove and a wide area off the cradles of the Shipyard provided a hockey and skating surface for about ten days. Often boys would venture out to the middle of the harbour where a channel was kept open by running intermittent trips of the

Ferry Between Dartmouth and Halifax.

No. 31

SEASON TICKET, terminating 30th June 1850.

AND SUBJECT TO THE GENERAL REGULATIONS.

THIS TICKET

Entitles to pass the Ferry as often as the Steamers may run :

Man and wife, unmarried children being minors, domestic Servants, and a One Horse Vehicle, owned by the proprietor of this Ticket. The privilege not covering the Lumber trade, or any business employing Teams constantly.

PROPRIETOR OF THIS TICKET. *J E Lawler*
Persons to Pass :

Edw H Lowe
Agent & Manager.

A ferry pass like this one from 1850 would have been used by hockey players travelling between Halifax and Dartmouth to enjoy games on the lakes or the North West Arm.

The Halifax and Dartmouth ferries have operated since 1752 and have provided Halifax residents with easy access to Dartmouth's lakes for hockey and skating during the winter months.

ferry throughout the day and night. By the first of February all three boats had their paddle-wheels so badly damaged that they abandoned the ice-battle. For the next three days, a tug-boat performed a slow and uncertain pedestrian service, but vehicular traffic was at a complete standstill. Many Halifax families went without milk.[33]

With its many lakes and the new downtown locks, Dartmouth was attracting an increasing number of visitors, and the convenience of the ferry service helped. On January 1, 1830, the *Sir Charles Ogle*, the first steamboat built in Canada, was launched in Dartmouth as a Halifax-Dartmouth ferry. Its predecessor, powered by a team of horses, often took an hour to cross the harbour, whereas the *Ogle* could complete the trip in seven minutes. With nearly all Halifax citizens at the time confined to dwellings situated on streets fronting the harbour, it quickly became a popular practice for working people and their families to travel to Dartmouth for recreation, especially on Sunday afternoons. Liquor was obtainable on the Dartmouth side, which also added to the popularity of the trip. Halifax tipplers who came for that purpose remained until late at night. Even the ferrymen sometimes took advantage of this perk as reported in 1831, when an intoxicated ferry captain's boat capsized and fourteen passengers drowned.[34]

Eager to get out on the ice in the winter months, the local population used whatever mode of transportation available to get to the lakes. In 1863, *The Halifax Reporter* described the new omnibus service between Province Building (Province House) and Chocolate Lake in Armdale:

Dartmouth's Lake Banook has been a popular winter recreation area for centuries. In this circa-1900 photo, curlers and skaters enjoy the natural ice surface.

We are glad to learn that, in accordance with a hint thrown out in the Reporter a few days ago, the Messrs. Conlon have decided, until further notice, to run an omnibus between the Province Building and Chocolate Lake (while the skating holds good) starting from the former place at 2 o'clock, p.m. The Messrs. C. are old servants of the travelling public, to whom they have always given the greatest satisfaction, and we trust that their enterprise in the present case will meet with its just reward.

One week later, further information was provided:

Conlon has changed their hour of running the busses to Chocolate Lake, from 2 to half-past two, p.m. His charge is only twenty-five cents and twelve and a half for return. If the skating parties will only patronize him liberally, we have no doubt the fare will be reduced a quarter for both ways. Don't let the enterprise fail, now that it is taken in hand.[35]

The North West Arm, an extension of Halifax Harbour, which forms the western boundary of peninsular Halifax, was a popular location for skating and hockey in the 1800s. In the background is the Memorial Tower, which was erected in 1912 to celebrate the introduction of representative government in Nova Scotia.[36] Global warming and water pollution have prevented the arm from freezing in recent years.

Two years later, on March 13, 1865, the *Acadian Recorder* complained about road conditions to the lakes in Dartmouth:

> If our friends over the water are desirous of seeing their Halifax neighbours during the skating season they would do well to pay a little more attention to the state of the roads....The roads to the Lakes are in a very bad state and a few loads of good solid material would make them much more pleasant to travelers.[37]

As the settlement continued to grow, skating continued to gain in popularity. Describing Halifax/Dartmouth's favourite winter pastime, the newspapers reported:"the lakes were thronged by a multitude of skaters" (*The Halifax Reporter*, January 13, 1863). The following week, the enthusiasm continued:

> The skating on the Arm, on Thursday last, was Truly Magnificent and the place was visited by a very large number of both sexes. It is thought that the ice may not be much injured by the rain of yesterday.[38]

They were correct about the ice; a few days later, this comment appeared in The *Halifax Reporter*:"The North West Arm was crowded these few days past by pleasure seekers who found the ice beautiful."[39] But skating on the arm or the harbour was not without its risks, as noted in an article from 1865:

> A Gallant Rescue. On Friday afternoon some hundreds of persons visited the Arm for the purpose of skating, the ice in some portions being sufficiently strong and smooth for that purpose. Late in the afternoon, a young lady who had incautiously ventured too near the edge of a headland where the surface was thin, suddenly fell through, in water some eight or ten feet deep. Numbers rushed to the rescue; but the greatest credit is due to the intrepidity and bravery of an officer of the 17th Regiment—Capt. Grant—who, without the slightest hesitation, plunged into the opening in the ice, and kept the young lady afloat. The situation was a very precarious one, as the latter was fast succumbing to the cold and fright. Rails and sticks were procured, and finally, after being some ten minutes in the water, all parties were safely got to land, numerous others crowding around having in the meantime fallen in. All present consider that the young lady had a very narrow escape from drowning; and her preserver is entitled to more than a passing notice of his meritorious deed.[40]

Still, the local population could not be persuaded to give up their recreations on the ice. As evidenced by the appearance of the following poem on the front page of the January 20, 1863, edition of The *Halifax Reporter*, they looked forward to the return of winter and the chance to put their skates on again:

"Frost"

The time of Frost is the time for me.
When the gay blood spins through the heart with glee;
When the voice leaps out with a chiming sound,
And the footstep rings on the musical ground;
When the earth is gray, and the air is bright;
And every breath a new delight!

Hurra! the lake is a league of grass!
Buckle and strap on the stiff white glass.
Off we shoot, and poise and wheel;
And swiftly turn upon scoring heel;
And our flying sandals chirp and sing
Like a flock of swallows gay on the wing.

 Happy skaters! jubilant flight!
Easily leaning to left and right,
Curving, coasting an islet of aware,
Balancing sharp on the glassy cord
With single foot,—ah, wretch unshriven!
A new star dawns in the fishes' heaven.

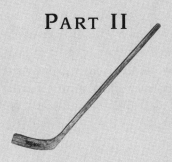

PART II

HOCKEY TAKES HOLD

With so many energetic people in search of recreation, with so many different games being played in one area, with an infrastructure and a social network to encourage play, and with an array of lakes and ponds nearby, the various games played by local residents were naturally brought out onto the ice. Because there are so few detailed descriptions of early hockey and so many different names for the game, however, it is difficult to pinpoint when hockey was first played and how exactly it evolved. What can be said with confidence is that a form of hockey was played in Halifax/Dartmouth as early as the 1820s, probably even earlier, and regularly by the early 1830s—earlier than anywhere else to date. The use of ice skates and hockey sticks helps to differentiate hockey from its precursors, and by the 1860s, the term "hockey" was used exclusively to describe the increasingly popular game.

"MIC-MAC" HOCKEY STICKS Hardware & Metal April 18 1906

Made of selected second growth yellow birch, for forwards and defence, the natural grain of wood running with curve of the blade. It possesses many advantages over the steam bent stick. Some of its excellent features are :—1st, Stiffness and Lightness. 2nd, Will not fray at bottom of blade. 3rd, Keeps its correct shape. 4th, Correct in pattern and weight. 5th, Every Stick carefully inspected before leaving factory. The attention of Dealers and Manufacturers is drawn to the fact that our hockey sticks are fully covered at Ottawa, viz.: the words "MIC-MAC" and "REX" as Trade Marks and the designs of the REX as an industrial design. Infringers will be prosecuted.

Starr Mfg. Co.
LIMITED
DARTMOUTH, N.S.
Toronto Branch :
126 WELLINGTON ST., W.

Perhaps it was from seeing the Mi'kmaw winter game being played that immigrants and military men came up with the idea of moving their field games onto the ice. Or perhaps the long winters and the sheer quantity of smooth ice surfaces made such a transition obvious. Regardless, games were played on the ice in Nova Scotia in the eighteenth and early nineteenth centuries. For clues to illustrate the point, Dr. Bruce Fergusson looked to the writings of Thomas Chandler Haliburton, a Nova Scotian lawyer, member of the Legislative Assembly, judge, and creator of the fictional character Sam Slick. In this quotation from *The Attaché*, a fictional work published in 1844, Dr. Fergusson finds reference to the game of hurley being played on the ice:

> ...But, oh dear me! If this piece of home happens to be an old schoolfeller, don't it awaken idees not only of home, but idees long since forgotten of old times? Memory acts on thought like heat on a dormant fly, it wakes it from the dead, puts new life into it, and it stretches out its wings and buzzes round as if it had never slept. When you see him, don't the old schoolmaster rise up before you as natural as if it was only yesterday? And the school-room, and the noisy, larkin, happy holidays, and you boys let out racin', yelpin', hollerin', and whoopin' like mad with pleasure, and the playground, and the game at bass [base, i.e. Rounders] in the field, or hurley on the long pond on the ice, or campin' out a-night at Chester lakes to fish—[1]

The setting for this scene, a reminiscence of Haliburton's youth, is King's College School in Windsor, Nova Scotia, circa 1810. Interestingly—and problematically—more than twenty-five years after Dr. Fergusson used the Haliburton quotation to show that sports were regularly played in Nova Scotia (thirty-five years, in fact, after Dr. Martin first made reference to it)[2], it was cited as evidence that hockey was played in Windsor around 1800.

Although hockey was, at times, referred to as "hurley" because of a resemblance between the sticks used in the two games, such was probably not the case until the 1830s or 40s. Hurling or hurley is a popular Irish field sport, invented in the second or third century and formerly played by various Celtic peoples. The goal of the game is to carry the slitter (ball) on a hurley (a stick with a narrow shaft about three feet long with a wide, curved blade), to the other team's goal. The slitter has a circumference of nine to ten inches. Played in a rough manner, the game of hurley resembles lacrosse, and is still played today, mainly in Ireland.[3] *Chambers's Information for the People* (1848) provides a good description of the game Irish immigrants in Halifax, Dartmouth, and Windsor would have played in the early nineteenth century:

> The forms of the game are these:—The players, sometimes to the number of fifty or sixty, being chosen for each side, they are arranged (usually barefoot) in two opposing ranks, with their

DR. C. BRUCE FERGUSSON
1911–1978

Born in Port Morien, Cape Breton, in 1911, Bruce Fergusson graduated from Nova Scotia Normal College, where he received the Governor General's Award for academic achievement. He continued his studies at Dalhousie, winning numerous scholarships, a bachelor of arts degree, and a diploma with distinction in history, English, and philosophy. As a Rhodes Scholar, Dr. Fergusson attended Oxford University and obtained three degrees—honours B.A., M.A. and D. Phil. While at Oxford, he won the half-blue for hockey. Provincial archivist from 1957 until his retirement in 1977, he had been a member of the Canadian Historical Association and the Nova Scotia Historic Sites Advisory Council, and chairman of the Historic Sites and Monuments Board of Canada.[4] Clearly, the late Dr. Fergusson had a passion for both hockey and history.

Dr. Bruce Fergusson, second from left, front row, with fellow members of the Historic Sites and Monuments Board of Canada, 1964.

hurleys crossed, to await the tossing up of the ball, the wickets or goals being previously fixed at the extremities of the hurling-green, which, from the nature of the play, is required to be a level extensive plain. Then there are two picked men chosen to keep the goal on each side, over whom the opposing party places equally tried men as a counterpoise; the duty of these goal-keepers being to arrest the ball in case of its near approach to that station, and return it back towards that of the opposite party, while those placed over them exert all their energies to drive it through the wicket. All preliminaries being adjusted, the leaders take their places in the centre. A person is chosen to throw up the ball, which is done as straight as possible, when the whole party, withdrawing their hurleys, stand with them elevated, to receive and strike it in its descent: now comes the crash of mimic war—hurleys rattle against hurleys—the ball is struck and restruck, often for several minutes, with advancing much more nearer to either goal; and when some one is lucky enough to get a clear "puck" at it, it is sent flying over the field. It is now followed by the entire party at their utmost speed; the men grapple, wrestle, and toss each other with amazing agility, neither victor nor vanquished waiting to take breath, but following the course of the rolling and flying prize; the best runners watch each other, and keep almost shoulder to shoulder through the play, and the best wrestlers keep as close on them as possible, to arrest or impede their progress. *The ball must not be taken from the ground by hand; and the tact and skill shown in taking it on the point of the hurley, and running with it half the length of the field, and, when too closely pressed, striking it towards the goal, is a matter of astonishment to those who are but slightly acquainted with the play.* At the goal is the chief brunt of the battle. The goal-keepers receive the prize, and are opposed by those set over them: the struggle is tremendous—every power of strength and skill is exerted: while the parties from opposite sides of the field run at full speed to support their men engaged in the conflict: then the tossing and straining are at their height, the men often lying in dozens side by side on the grass, *while the ball is returned by some strong arm again, flying above their heads, towards the other goal* [emphasis added].[5]

Besides the fact that in hurley the ball is played primarily in the air, the Haliburton quotation does not mention whether or not the boys are wearing skates, the very minimum of the criteria that makes hockey different from hurley. It is the attempt to find historical fact in a fictional work, however, that is the most serious fallacy. A fictional work cannot be expected to substantiate claims about actual historical events. Dr. Fergusson was appropriately cautious in the use he made of this fictional material. As the SIHR notes in their report, "For one thing, he sees it only as a clue that hurley 'was played on ice in Nova Scotia in the eighteenth century'; for another, he avoids conveying any notion that the clue represents the beginning of hurley on the ice."[6]

When the Nova Scotia Department of Transportation erected the "birthplace of hockey" sign outside of the town in the 1990s, it ignored the opinion held by many of the province's most reputed historians that hockey originated in Dartmouth and Halifax. (Interestingly, the claim of Cooperstown, New York, as the birthplace of baseball is subject to a similar controversy in the United States.[7]) Bill Fitsell, hockey historian from Kingston, Ontario, explains:

> Windsor has slim evidence of any stick ball game being played there throughout the mid 1800's. That's not the case in the Halifax area. And that's the rub. Windsor's aggressive promotion has taken the limelight away from [the] Dartmouth-Halifax area, where there are numerous citations of ice games being played and reported on the following day in the press. Windsor has not produced such next day reports in the early or mid 1800's. The Windsor enthusiasts have "taken coal to Newcastle" in publicizing their birthplace claims and have ignored the strong roots of Halifax and Dartmouth.[8]

Renowned Dartmouth artist Tom Forrestall, an Officer of the Order of Canada, has been painting scenes of hockey and other sports on the Dartmouth lakes for many years. He is not the first artist to capture the games being played: in the 1870s, H.B. Laurence painted winter activities on Lake Banook.

WINDSOR, NOVA SCOTIA

Home to Shand House Museum, Fort Edward Blockhouse, Hants County Exhibition (the oldest agricultural fair in Canada), King's Edgehill (the oldest private educational institution in the British Commonwealth), and the estate of renowned writer Thomas Chandler Haliburton, Windsor, Nova Scotia, is a wonderful old town with an interesting and unique history. Recently, Howard Dill's famous giant pumpkins and the Mermaid Theatre have gained international prominence. Unfortunately, however, Windsor has tried to add "the birthplace of hockey" to this list—a claim that cannot be substantiated by the existing historical records.

Furthermore, some of Windsor's supporting evidence does not appear to be historically accurate. For example, the Windsor Hockey Heritage Society claims that Windsor became known as the "playground of Halifax" in the 1800s, reasoning that "many King's students were from the Halifax/Dartmouth area, so ice hurley naturally spread there first."[9] Significantly, however, the first regular stagecoach service in Nova Scotia did not operate until 1816, when two weekly trips from Halifax to Windsor carried six passengers each. The route to Windsor was at least ninety kilometers, and the operator Isaiah Smith had to change the horses every 24 kilometers. The fare between these two points was $6—a considerable amount of money at the time. I have been unable to determine the time it took to make this trip, but the mail delivery from Halifax to Windsor took over two days by horseback in 1828.[10] Nowhere in the course of my research did I come across a reference to Windsor as the "playground of Halifax." In fact, the town of Dartmouth is most often mentioned as the favoured locale for swimming, skating, hockey, and other winter and summer pastimes.

The Birthplace of Hockey sign

To escape crowded Halifax for the country air, many successful businessmen of the 1800s moved to Dartmouth. These men included the Hon. Joseph Howe, the Hon. John E. Fairbanks, John Prescott Mott, who made his fortune in the chocolate business, the Hon. Dr. Parker, the Hon. Justice James William Johnstone, and John Esdaile, a retired Montreal merchant. In 1854, Howe lamented the difficulty of the journey from the Annapolis Valley to Halifax in an effort to garner support for a railway line:

> I have at this moment a daughter—the last, perhaps, that may be left to me—dear to me as the apple of my eye—residing 70 miles distant and whom I have not seen for 6 months. Why? Because I have no means of going there rapidly and returning to attend to the public business which daily presses on me.[11]

The unsatisfactory roadway to Windsor was also a key factor in the effort to build the Shubenacadie Canal. Until the railway was completed, it was cheaper to transport produce and other commodities around the province by sea from Windsor to Halifax, a distance of three hundred miles, rather than by traveling the overland route of only sixty miles. As a result, many New England sea captains built large fortunes from this coastal trade. After becoming an object of partisan politics, the railroad to Windsor was completed on June 3, 1858. Finally, residents of Halifax and Dartmouth could proceed with relative ease to Windsor to share their favourite winter pastimes, like hockey, which by that time was well-established in Halifax/Dartmouth.

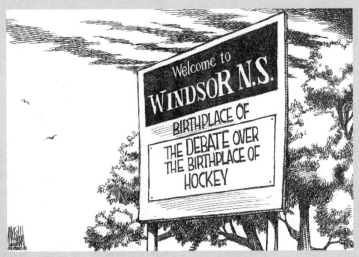

Bruce MacKinnon, The Sunday Herald, *June 16, 2002.*

During the nineteenth century, silhouette portraits were popular among the wealthy citizens of Great Britain, America, and the Colonies. In the winter of 1830-31, silhouettist Hankes cut profiles in Halifax that were notable for their fine execution. Working with "great rapidity but rare skill and delicacy," he charged half a dollar for adults and half-price for children. From his studio in the large upper room of the Exchange Coffee House and the City Court House, Hankes cut portraits for many important people in the town, including the governor, Sir Peregrine Maitland. This silhouette of William and Elizabeth Piers and their six-year-old son, Henry, clearly shows the young boy holding his hockey stick. Henry recalled as an adult that Hankes "worked exceedingly rapidly, cutting out the portrait with scissors directly from the sitter, without any preliminary drawing or the aid of subsidiary appliances that were sometimes used by less expert men." Hankes closed his gallery, which was known as a "papyrotomia," shortly after completing these silhouettes.[12]

Stephen Coutts, manager of operations and collections at the Nova Scotia Sport Hall of Fame, holds an antique hockey stick in the same manner as young Henry Piers. Although the size of the stick is magnified in the shadow, the similiarity between the two sticks confirms that the stick Henry was holding in 1830-31 was indeed a hockey stick.

EARLY NAMES FOR THE GAME

Some of the confusion surrounding our early ice hockey history has resulted because elements of the various games and the terms used to describe them were borrowed and mixed—just as the cultural groups themselves were intermingling. As noted, "hurley" was the name of the Irish field sport and the stick used by players of this sport. From the 1830s until about the 1850s, however, "hurley" (or "hurly") referred to the game of hockey as well as the sticks used in it.[13]

For evidence of the connection between hurley and hockey, Dr. Fergusson turns to an 1887 issue of the *Dalhousie Gazette*, in which a Dalhousie alumnus remembers and describes the ice game commonly played at the university from 1838 to 1843:

> Baseball came in with the Mayflowers and did not last much longer. It was only played in Spring, but in Winter the common and almost only game was then called hurly, but now known as hockey. It was played either on foot on land, or on skates on ice. The latter required much the greater skill.[14]

By noting that a game called "hurly" was played "on skates on ice," the speaker makes it clear that in the 1830s the word "hurley" (or "hurly") had begun to refer to the game "now known as hockey." In 1859, *The British Colonist* reported on January 4:

> The Young Men of Halifax
>
> We have long held the opinion that the young men of this city are second to none in the world for energy, skill and daring, in all manly games and exercises;
>
> Often have we been led to express the same opinion, when the bat laid aside, skates strapped on, and hurly in hand, the ball is followed over the glassy surface of the lakes, which ring to the skates' heel...[15]

The "hurly in hand" following the ball over the ice was clearly a hockey stick. As previously noted, the traditional hurley was used to carry or propel the ball in the air.

The terms wicket and ricket were also used, for a brief time at least, when referring to the game of hockey. Noting the use of the word "wicket"—the name commonly used for the goal posts—to signify an early form of hockey, Dr. Fergusson referred to a newspaper report from *The Novascotian* in 1831:

> Winter Sports—The weather, during the past week or ten days, has been delightful: generally clear, with an unclouded sky, and singularly

moderate for the season. There has been excellent skating upon the head of the North West Arm, and large parties of our Townsfolk and the Military, have enjoyed, during several afternoons of this and the past week, the healthy and spirit stirring game of Wicket.[16]

In 1842, the *Halifax Morning Post* reported on a game described as ricket, also apparently so named after the goal posts:

> Skating—The Dartmouth lakes were rough yesterday, Maynard's was best—but a good spot might be found on almost any of them for a game of ricket. By the way, there is to be a great match today, if the weather be fine—which is very doubtful.[17]

The 1895 Standard Dictionary of the English Language *describes the skate as "a contrivance consisting usually of a keel-like runner attached to a plate or frame, with suitable clamps or straps for fastening it to the sole of a boot or shoe, enabling the wearer to glide rapidly over the ice." Illustrations include an early bone skate to "an American club skate." The claim that Dartmouth's Starr skate plant was the best in the world was not exaggerated. The modern "American club skate" illustrated in the dictionary was in fact the Starr Acme Club skate which revolutionized skate design.*

Dr. Martin's *The Story of Dartmouth* contains what I believe to be the most significant proof with respect to the advanced state of the game of hockey in Dartmouth in the 1840s. The information contained in a ten-page excerpt from the diary of a Mrs. Gould was first highlighted by Dr. Martin in his 1955 article, "The Birthplace of Hockey."[18] He noted that Mrs. Gould appeared to possess a photographic memory, describing her narrative as "invaluable…a veritable mine of information concerning life in our village during the first half of the last century."[19] Published in 1900 in the *Windsor Hants Journal*, Mrs. Gould's memoirs included the following proof that hockey, or ricket, was played on Lake Banook in the 1840s:

> The Dartmouth Lakes and the small ponds were the only resorts of skaters and ricket players—the game now known as hockey. Men and boys came over from Halifax to the First Lake [Banook] in large numbers on fine afternoons. Among the men, the face of Robert, or James Moran, merchant, always healthful and rosy-looking: and among the younger men, Jimmy Duffus, as he was known, come up before me now. Young Duffus had fine clothes, fur cap and gauntlets, and above all a pair of spring skates. Consequently he always had other Halifax boys with him. Mr. Moran loved skating as an exercise, and the same can be said of Mr. John McNab, who in later years was drowned, I think, in Halifax harbor. He excelled in figure and fancy skating. He was always against Dan Murphy, a Dartmouth champion, in the ricket and hockey matches. William Foster, senior, the cigar manufacturer, was fond of the game, and always stood ricket guard with his creepers [i.e. soft-soled shoes] on, as he was not a skater.[20]

Not only does Mrs. Gould refer to the game as "ricket," one of the most common names for hockey in the 1840s, she confirms that ricket was "the game now known as hockey." Significantly, she also confirms that goaltenders were used and that the players wore skates.

⌒

HOCKEY: HERE TO STAY

By the late 1850s, the word "hockey" was beginning to enter the lexicon of the game, although "ricket" continued to be used occasionally until the 1870s; on January 22, 1873, for example, the article "Skating on the N.W. Arm" in *The Acadian Reporter* commented: "and then again it was amusing to see the zeal displayed by men and boys in trying to be the conquerors in a game of Ricket…"[21] By whatever name it was called, hockey had taken hold as the winter game of choice for Halifax/Dartmouth sports enthusiasts by the mid-1800s. Dr. Fergusson notes that early in 1864, the Halifax newspapers had begun debating the advantages and disadvantages of hockey. *The Halifax Reporter* declared on January 2:

> If we turn towards the country, we are at once struck by the almost
> total absence of stone throwing boys, upon whose characteristics

and mode of life we remarked in a former article. What has become of them? The nearest pond answers this question; they are playing hockey on the ice and occasionally mimicking the mistakes of such among their betters as are not quite at home upon skates.[22]

In *The Halifax Morning Sun* of January 25, 1864, the writer of "Hints on Skating" lamented the ever increasing popularity of the sport:

> Hockey…ought to be sternly forbidden 'as it is not only annoying but dangerous. In its right place, hockey is a noble game, and deserving of every encouragement, but on the ice it is in its wrong place, and should be prohibited. The game, moreover, is by no means what it ought to be, inasmuch as it is impossible to enforce the rules in such a miscellaneous assembly. No one keeps to any particular side, or aims at any particular goal; and anyone who happens to have a stick hits the ball in any direction that seems easiest…[23]

The game of hockey, with its speed and action on skates, was obviously a dramatic sight for the relatively staid skaters of the day. To those unfamiliar with it, hockey appeared to be a haphazard game played among "a miscellaneous assembly"; according to Dr. Fergusson, however, "part of this criticism applied to practice rather than to a real hockey match."[24]

The following newspaper report from February 17, 1867, proved to Dr. Martin's satisfaction that hockey was a long-established sport in Dartmouth. Indeed, this detailed description of early hockey in Halifax/Dartmouth, which equates ricket with hockey, meets the "six defining characteristics" of the SIHR definition—"ice surface, two contesting teams, players on skates, use of curved sticks, small propellant, objective of scoring on opposite goals"[25]:

> On Saturday there were about 1,500 people at Oathill Lake. Two well contested games of ricket were being played at the upper end of the lake where a number of young men from Dartmouth and the City were playing their hurleys and "following up" the ball. The centre of the lake was occupied by a number of officers of the Garrison and the Fleet in a match game called hockey, i.e., ricket.
>
> Very little science was displayed in either game, the old class of players seems to have died out, and their successors are not up to the science of leading off the ball, doubling and carrying it through. Instead of the old style, the game as now played is dangerous to outsiders especially the ladies, some of whom were rather roughly treated in the scrimmages after the ball.[26]

Although the language in the description of the game above is somewhat out of date, it signifies actions that are clearly those of the game of hockey, such as stick-handling ("doubling,")[27] and scoring ("carrying it through"). Significantly, by

1867, when this article was written, the game's history was long enough for it to have had an old and a new style of game and class of players. The sport continued to be played and grow in popularity throughout the century. By 1900, ice hockey was as familiar in most parts of Canada as it was in the 1840s to Mrs. Gould of Dartmouth.

In Halifax: Warden of the North, Governor General's Award winner and historian Thomas Raddall writes:

> It is a fact little known in Canada, but a fact none the less, that ice-hockey, Canada's national game, began on the Dartmouth lakes in the eighteenth century. Here the garrison officers found the Indians playing a primitive form of hurley on the ice, adopted and adapted it, and later put the game on skates. When they were transferred to military posts along the St. Lawrence and the Great Lakes they took the game with them and for some time afterwards continued to send to the Dartmouth Indians for the necessary sticks.[28]

Although the exact time and manner in which hockey was born in Halifax and Dartmouth is unclear, there is no doubt that the new game played an important role in the winter recreation of the residents of the area. Having invented the new sport of hockey, Halifax/Dartmouth's continued influence on the game was inevitable.

PART III

STICKS, SKATES AND STARR

Naturally, the proliferation of hockey in Halifax and Dartmouth had an impact on the equipment required for this new winter pastime. To properly enjoy the new game, players would require its most important implements—sticks and skates. And the area produced the finest sticks and skates available anywhere. This fact ensured the growth of the game both locally and abroad as other parts of Canada and the world soon caught on to this exciting new game on ice.

THE FIRST HOCKEY STICKS

There is no doubt that the Mi'kmaq had an important influence on the game of ice hockey as it developed in Halifax/Dartmouth. The local Mi'kmaw population not only played a game on ice that may have inspired the modern-day game of hockey, they also played an important role in the development of the hockey stick. The early hockey sticks (or "hurleys") were made at the Mi'kmaq encampment at Tuft's Cove and on Lake MicMac in Dartmouth. In "Hockey in the Old Days," Dr. Martin asserts that: "Making hurleys was quite a business with the Indians at the Tuft's Cove encampment or at those bordering the lakes. Isaac Cope, member of the well known MicMac [Mi'kmaq] who lived at Second Red Bridge [Lake Mic Mac] for so many years, and who died at the Truro reservation only re-

Popular Dartmouth hockey coach and teacher Paul Barry displays his family's antique hockey stick from the 1800s. Hand-carved from a single tree root, the stick came from Paul's grandfather's home in Dartmouth. The family's ancestors came to Dartmouth when the Shubenacadie Canal was being constructed in the early 1800s. Paul's grandfather worked in Dartmouth's ice industry, while his father, Allan, was president of the Dartmouth Minor Hockey Association in the early 1970s.

cently, once told me that for years his people made hundreds of hurleys from the woods around Lake MicMac every season. They were shipped all over the Maritimes, and even to Montreal. One of the biggest buyers locally was the Starr Manufacturing Company, who wholesaled them to the hardware merchants hereabouts, and shipped large quantities to their branch office in Toronto."[1]

Local stick manufacturing would have a significant impact on the growth of hockey in Montreal and Kingston. Montreal merchant Harry Joseph, a friend of Halifax's J.G.A. Creighton, recalled in a 1936 interview that they obtained hockey sticks from Halifax and Dartmouth for the first games in Montreal in 1875. He noted: "Prior to that year, I had never seen a hockey stick around Montreal, nor seen hurley or shinny played on skates."[2]

Players in Kingston also relied on Halifax and Dartmouth sticks for their early games. In an 1895 article,

William H. Kerr advised that some of his fellow senior cadets reported that Halifax made "simply wonderful sticks" so an order was made for the first Kingston games. "Such beauties as they were…made out of small trees planed down, with roots for blades; warranted irresistible by any shin."[3]

Starr advertisements touting "strong and accurate" Rex and MicMac hockey sticks appeared in newspapers commencing in the 1860s. Subsequent ads, like the one below from 1908, would contain more details:

Rex Hockey Sticks

Our latest pattern, made of straight grain selected second growth yellow birch. For Expert Players. Longitudinal serrations on handle ensuring firm grip and preventing sticks slipping from player's hands. Double grooved blade, the lower one also serrated. This enables the puck to be accurately shot for goal and strengthens the stick at its weakest point. The word 'Rex' is covered at Ottawa. Infringers will be prosecuted.[4]

In the late 1930s, noted Dartmouth hockey player Col. B.A. Weston (then in his eighties) stated that it was his understanding that the Mi'kmaq "played the game on the Dartmouth lakes long before the sixties. The hockey sticks, which differed slightly from those in use today, were made by the Indians, who make them today, and it may not be generally known that for many years sticks manufactured by these Indians have been shipped from here to the Upper Provinces and the United States."[5] Weston, who played hockey on the Dartmouth Lakes with the Mi'kmaq in the 1860s and confirmed their use of wooden pucks, was later elected president of the Dartmouth Amateur Athletic Association.

In 1943, sports writer Frank Power reported in *The Halifax Mail* that William Gill, a talented scenic artist from Halifax who moved to Boston, believed that hockey was first played on the North West Arm in Halifax. The following quotation from

Gill not only confirmed the source of the sticks, but confirmed the fact that goal-tenders were used locally:

> I always played goal. Previous to the rubber puck, which came in
> about 1872, I made my own dead round ball. The first sticks came
> from the Indians. I had more than one—bought them at the Green
> Market.[6]

Although the Tuft's Cove encampment was destroyed by the Halifax Explosion in 1917, Mi'kmaq in the area continued to manufacture hockey sticks well into the 1930s.[7]

THE STARR SPRING SKATE:
A REVOLUTION IN SKATING

Given the ever-growing popularity of skating and hockey in Halifax and Dartmouth, it is not surprising that the demand for skates was to be met with the supply of a product that was unsurpassed at the time and for many years thereafter—the Starr spring skate.

The construction of the Shubenacadie Canal had not only provided an influx of young, skilled workers who settled in Dartmouth and played hockey and other sports on its many lakes, it also provided water power for industrial use in the town. In 1861, the Starr Manufacturing Company, which was named after founder and businessman John Starr, entered into an agreement with The Inland Navigation Company, owners of the Shubenacadie Canal, to use the water that flowed from Sullivan's Pond to Halifax Harbour. This water would be run through a separate flume to power a turbine that would operate machinery for the production of nuts, bolts, and nails. The plant was located in an old shed used as a gold crusher. Quickly, however, the primary focus of the company would change.

In 1861, John Forbes was hired as the foreman for the new company. In 1842, at the age of eight, John Forbes had left for Nova Scotia with his family, artisans from Birmingham, England. His father, William Forbes, was a watchmaker. As a young man, Forbes worked in a hardware store in Halifax and sold old-fashioned skates.[8]

For many centuries, wood frame skates, which were simply strapped to the boot, were the only type of skate available. Subsequently, a wooden frame skate that was fastened with two leather straps had a screw that went into the heel of the boot .The first all-metal skates, developed in the middle of the nineteenth century, had brass plates at toe and heel, and corresponding plates were inset in the sole and heel-tap of shoes. The plates engaged and locked with a pin. In the next improvement, the heel-plate turned up as a lug at the back of the boot. A small thumb-screw passed through a lug into the metal nut set in the back of the boot

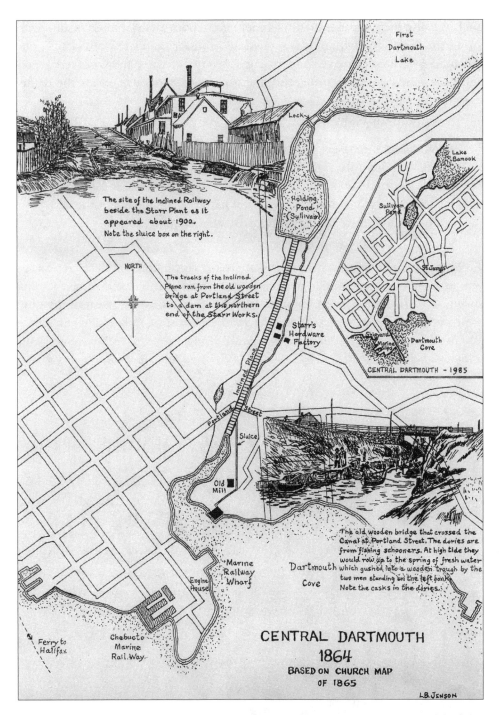

The site of the Inclined Railway beside the Starr Plant as it appeared about 1900. Note the sluice box on the right.

NORTH

The tracks of the Inclined Plane ran from the old wooden bridge at Portland Street to a dam at the northern end of the Starr Works.

First Dartmouth Lake

Lock

Lake Banook

Holding Pond (Sullivan)

Sullivan Pond

St James

Starr's Hardware Factory

Shipyard
Marine Slip

Dartmouth Cove

CENTRAL DARTMOUTH - 1985

Portland Inclined Plane

Portland Street

Sluice

Old Mill

The old wooden bridge that crossed the Canal at Portland Street. The dories are from fishing schooners. At high tide they would row up to the spring of fresh water which gushed into a wooden trough by the two men standing on the left bank. Note the casks in the dories.

Dartmouth Cove

Marine Railway Wharf

Engine House

Ferry to Halifax

Chebucto Marine Rail.Way

CENTRAL DARTMOUTH
1864
BASED ON CHURCH MAP
OF 1865

L.B.JENSON

This diagram illustrates the close relationship between the Starr Plant in Dartmouth and the adjacent Shubenacadie Canal. The inclined plane was used to transport canal boats to the first lock at Sullivan's Pond and the canal's water provided a power source for the plant. A residential development is being planned for most of this historic canal and Starr plant site.

heel.[9] Clearly, these methods of attachment were both awkward and insufficient.

In the early 1860s, there was a great demand for skates in both Halifax and Dartmouth. Various local newspapers, published two or three times per week, generally contained at least two advertisements per issue for skates during the winter months:

> Skates for the Millions
>
> Intending purchasers of skates, will consult their own interests, by calling at the store of the Subscriber, where can be found a large and well assorted stock, suitable for Ladies, Gents, Misses and Boys— comprising many new and beautiful patterns and also with the additional advantage of moderate prices to recommend them.
>
> John Bessonett [store, Halifax][10]

Forbes experimented with a new skate but his invention was delayed by a six-year term in America to obtain machine experience. In 1863, he made his famous spring skates with co-worker Thomas Bateman. The lever attachment of the newly patented skate was so much simpler than the existing skates that the spring skates "caught on like wildfire." In 1866, Starr brought out the Forbes Acme Skate, which was described in the 1875 edition of *Encyclopedia Britannica* as the best of any skate on the market.[11]

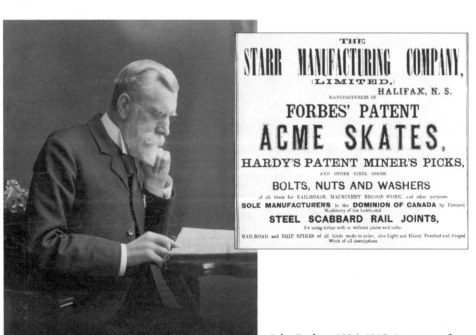

John Forbes, 1834-1915, inventor of the Starr Acme spring skate, which revolutionized skating and the game of ice hockey.

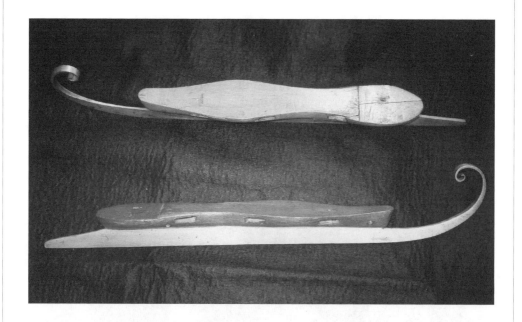

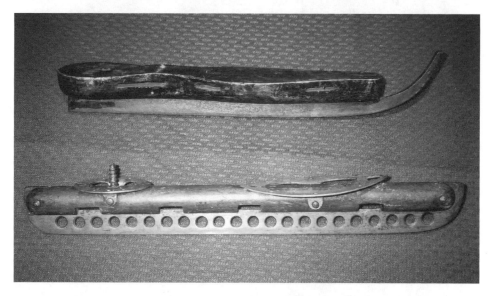

This photo illustrates the various types of skates available in the nineteenth century. Before the invention of the Starr spring skate in Dartmouth in 1863, skaters had to either strap (top image) or screw (bottom image) their skate blade to their boot. In 1848, Chambers's Information for the People *describes the skate as follows: "A skate is a well-known apparatus of wood and iron, with straps and buckles to attach it to the foot. The skate for each foot must be alike. The iron should not be deeper than three-quarters of an inch, and smooth or flat along its under edge: only boys' skates should be grooved, to take better hold of the ice. The iron should be a quarter of an inch thick. The edges should be smooth, free from rust, and sharply ground."*[12]

The Starr Manufacturing Company was soon exporting their new skates, out-selling their American and European competitors at the same time. *The Halifax Morning Chronicle* reported in 1866:

> A few days since Messrs. Starr shipped 40 packages of skates to Montreal, which were manufactured at Dartmouth. They have upwards of 20 men employed and turn out weekly large numbers of skates and hundreds of kegs of nails. The firm can manufacture skates cheaper than the article can be imported from England. Much of the apparatus used in the manufacture of the skates was invented by Mr. Forbes who is foreman of the works.[13]

Starr adds proclaimed: "Forbes Patent Acme Club Skate—The only reliable and really self-fastening skate ever invented. Can be instantly and firmly attached to any boot. No heel plates to clog up. No straps to lame the feet. Universally acknowledged."

By reducing the risk of having the wooden skate crack or the skate fall off the boot, the new Starr skate allowed skaters to make quicker and shorter turns, which meant hockey could for the first time be played on smaller ice surfaces, such as indoor rinks. The impact of the new skates was felt almost immediately, explains Dr. Martin:

> In the winter of 1867, Halifax newspapers carried unusually long accounts of seasonal activities on our lakes, such as games of curling, hockey and ice-boating. Up to about the mid-century there was only occasional reference to such recreations, perhaps because of the few persons participating. Now with a skate factory located in our midst, hundreds of others must have joined in the fashion. Increasing crowds came over from Halifax especially on holidays and Sundays. The bright uniforms of naval and military officers gliding over the glassy surfaces with their lady partners amid the throngs on our various lakes, created quite a colorful scene.
>
> The "Halifax Reporter" of that time observed that it was curious the way that skating enthusiasts of Halifax changed their location in different seasons. One year Maynard's Lake in Dartmouth has the

As confirmed by the signage on the factory, Starr skates became the star product shortly after the company opened in 1861.

STARR SKATES

Invented and produced at the Starr Manufacturing Plant in Dartmouth, Starr skates revolutionized hockey and ice skating. Made of metal, the new skates replaced the old wooden tops, which tended to split and were difficult to attach. Starr skates were sold under various names—Acme, MicMac, Scotia, Rideau, Demon, Regal, Bulldog, Acadia and Featherweight. A specific hockey skate was not patented until 1893-1895, a reflection of demand and the fact that hockey had become a popular sport outside of Halifax and Dartmouth. Before that time, the relatively small number of players and teams did not warrant specific marketing of a "made for hockey" product. This is confirmed by observing old hockey photographs—almost all the players wear Starr skates.

The influence of the Starr skate on hockey extended well into the twentieth century. In 1909, a Starr ad contained the following quote from "the famous hockey player" Dickey Boone: "I am most pleased to state that the hockey skates you manufacture have proved by factual use to embody the features wanted for that purpose. I cheerfully endorse your claims for them after personally using them." J.E. Eveleigh, captain of the

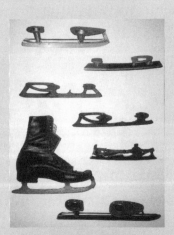

Montreal Hockey Team in 1908-1909, proclaimed: "I have tried them out and can sincerely say that I like them better than any I have used. They are light yet perfectly strong."[14] With millions of skates sold, Starr played an important role in popularizing hockey and skating around the world.

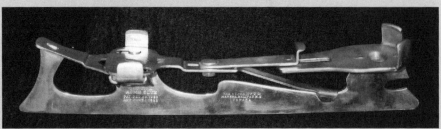

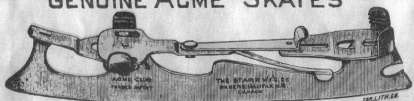

best ice; the next year the North West Arm will be the favorite: and another year First and Second Dartmouth Lake will bear the palm, said a writer of that day.[15]

For over seventy-five years, Dartmouth enjoyed a superior reputation because of the skate factory. Exhibits won gold medals at the Philadelphia Centennial Exposition of 1876, at the Chicago World's Fair of 1893, and at the Paris Exhibition of 1911. The Starr Company was also named skate makers to the royal house of Spain, by special appointment of King Alphonse XII.[16]

Booth of the Starr Manufacturing Company, Dartmouth, at the Nova Scotia Provincial Exhibition

Big display advertisements, often in French or German and featuring the latest styles and makes of skates, regularly appeared in ice-sport magazines of the United States and Canada. Leading newspapers throughout Canada sold plenty of space to the Starr Company, particularly during the fall and winter seasons. Dartmouthians abroad could not but be proud to learn of our local products in the columns of *La Patrie*, Montreal; *The Toronto World*; or *The Winnipeg Telegram*, for at the bottom of the advertisements, the notation would read:

The Starr Manufacturing Company, Ltd.
Works and Head Office, Dartmouth, N. S.
Branch office 122 Wellington St., Toronto[17]

In 1873, the governor general of Canada, Lord Dufferin, arrived in Halifax by government steamer. Lady Dufferin visited two important Dartmouth factories:

The whole party then proceeded by carriage to an inspection of the Ropeworks where they were shown through the plant by W. J. Stairs, the founder. Afterwards at the Starr Manufacturing Company Manager John Forbes presented Lady Dufferin with pairs of gold-plated skates for herself and Lord Dufferin. The party were then conveyed to Marshall's Inn at Porto Bello for an afternoon luncheon, after which they drove in to the mines at Montague to enthuse over activity there, and witness the process of gold crushing.[18]

In 1873, the Starr Manufacturing Company was at the peak of its prosperity with profits of $25,000. With the success of its skate, Starr was able to expand and diversify its business. They began to build coal cars, then built the first iron bridge in Nova Scotia and the golden gates at the entrance to Point Pleasant Park. In 1883, the company, under the supervision of John Forbes, made the two-hundred-foot swinging drawbridge section of the wooden train bridge that spanned Halifax Harbour. With over 250 employees, Forbes was making an annual salary of $2,000.[19] One of the employees in the latter part of the century was my great-uncle Dee. To this day, I am the proud owner of Uncle Dee's Starr Acme Spring Skates, which he would have obtained in the 1890s.

During the 1870s, Forbes amassed a fortune and built a large home, known as Lakeside, on Crichton Avenue. By 1874, an economic downturn resulted in a surplus of skates and a dividend could not be declared. The company's directors asked Forbes for the use of his patents, and by 1878, the company was once again profitable. Unfortunately, Forbes was dropped by the company in 1878. The Halifax newspapers reported: "Injustice suffered by father of great business—Those who profited by the products of his brains and the labors of his hands turned

The house in the upper right of the photo was built by John Forbes, inventor of the modern skate. The two stone pillars mark the entrance to the first canal lock.

In 1886, the Starr Manufacturing Company won a national competition to design and construct the golden gates for the entrance to Point Pleasant Park in Halifax. The gates, which have recently been restored, were a gift from Sir William Young, a former premier (1854) and chief justice (1860) of Nova Scotia.

against him." In his book on industry in Dartmouth, Harry Chapman notes that the patents of the company were allowed to lapse, which allowed the market to be flooded with cheap imitations of Starr skates. Meanwhile, Forbes left for Ontario and Chicago but returned to open his own company in direct competition with Starr. In 1898, Starr bought out Forbes and his patents and continued producing skates in what had become a very competitive market.[20]

Despite these problems, Starr continued to sell skates and build on its reputation of quality. Most early hockey photos show the players wearing Starr skates, and, as the game of hockey became more popular, endorsements from big name players and teams were common. In 1903, Harry C. DeWitt, Secretary of the Montreal Hockey Club, Champions of Canada, proclaimed: "Six out of seven men on our World's Championship team of last winter used the Starr Skates, and all are unanimous in the opinion that they exceed any other skate on the market, combining such essentials as lightness, durability and finish."[21] An advertisement from 1907 proclaimed: "Probably every prominent hockey player in Canada—for the past forty years—has used Starr Skates. Sixteen different styles, to suit all kinds of ice." This reputation was acknowledged throughout the country and, in fact, around the world. In 1908, the *Winnipeg Telegram* confirmed what Starr already knew: "Canada has the greatest skate factory in the world, and that factory is the Starr Manufacturing Company's works situated down by the sea at Dartmouth in the province of Nova Scotia."[22]

Making over eleven million skates, Starr continued their production into the 1930s. In 1937, the company sold more skates than any year previously, and the manager of the skate division reported that output would increase by more than twenty per cent. As Harry Chapman explains, the skate business would unfortunately not recover from the Great Depression:

> Dartmouth's economy was dealt a crippling blow in 1939, when
> Starr Manufacturing closed down the skate division. The product

had put the town on the international map. In spite of numerous favourable announcements by the company during the Depression years, Starr had let its patent renewal lapse and now faced stiff competition from inferior but cheaper German and American skates, which were flooding the international and local markets. In the past year, Starr had brokered a deal with Simpson's and Eaton's, two of Canada's largest department store chains at that time, whereby they bought large quantities of skates but at very low prices. Ontario boot-makers, such as Bauer of Kitchener, went into the skate-making business, creating more unwanted competition for the Nova Scotia plant. Closure of the skate factory marked the end of an important chapter in the town's industrial history, but more immediately in meant the loss of many jobs.[23]

Although Starr Manufacturing stopped making skates in 1939, its influence on our history continued. During the Second World War, the plant made rivets for ships, shell casings, and brackets for degaussing ships sailing out of Halifax Harbour. This de-magnetizing process protected the naval ships and merchant convoys from magnetic mines placed at the mouth of the harbour by German vessels. With many of its employees fighting overseas, the company replaced over eighty per cent of its workforce with female workers. In fact, because of the demands of the war years, the plant enjoyed its greatest production ever. With an additional three night shifts a week, the war helped Starr Manufacturing return to financial stability.[24]

The Starr factory continued to operate until 1996 making chrome furniture, plastic piping, nuts, bolts, and rivets, with its closing ending an important chapter in Dartmouth's industrial history. The Starr skates proudly displayed the name of the company and the name Halifax (though they were produced in the Dartmouth factory). I recently met a doctor, V. Gregus, in Dartmouth who had grown up in Slovakia. Although the skates they used were made in Eastern Europe, he told me that everyone referred to them as "Halifax skates." I subsequently learned that the Starr skates were the envy of one of the most famous figures from the twentieth century—Russian Marxist theorist and revolutionary Leon Trotsky, who wrote in his 1930 autobiography, *My Life*:

> Our relatives and friends, when going to town, would sometimes ask what I wanted from Elizavetgrad or Nikoloyev. My eyes would shine. What would I ask for? They would come to my help. One would suggest a toy horse, another books, another colored crayons, another a pair of skates. "I want half-Halifax skates!" I would cry, having heard this expression from my brother. But they would forget their promises as soon as they crossed the threshold. I lived in hope for several weeks, and then suffered a long disappointment.[25]

ADVERTISING HOCKEY

By the 1860s, as hockey grew in popularity in Dartmouth and Halifax, hockey and skating advertisements began to appear regularly in newspapers. Primarily from the Starr Manufacturing Company, these ads promoted skates and "Rex and MicMac hockey sticks," which, Starr advised, were "strong and accurate." As the century came to a close, the ads became more graphic, and soon endorsements from star hockey players complemented ads for skates and sticks. Alongside ads for hockey equipment, local newspapers advertised such products as "Dr. Buchan's sugar-coated Sarsaparilla Pills" and "Perry's Concentrated Detersive Essence." As hockey continued to rise in popularity, however, advertisers started using the game in their promotions. In 1903, for example, a merchant proclaimed: "The highest enthusiasm is aroused in a keenly contested game of Hockey. The highest expectations are realized in our Liquors."[26] A century of beer-and-hockey ads would soon follow!

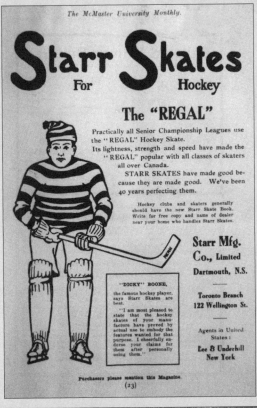

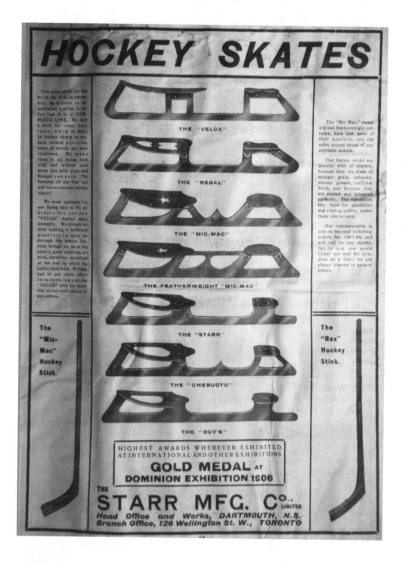

As part of its two-hundredth birthday celebrations in 1950, the city of Dartmouth, under the direction of Dr. John Martin, erected this plaque at the Starr Manufacturing Plant. Leander F. Stevens, who had been employed at the plant since 1883, participated in the ceremony. The plaque, which depicts both the spring skate and a more modern model, is now part of the collection of the Dartmouth Heritage Museum.

Although Trotsky may not have received his Starr skates, he did have a rather unexpected and eventful visit to Halifax. Returning home from New York to Russia to join the revolution in 1917, Trotsky's ship was intercepted. With his wife and two children, Trotsky stayed at the home of the Horowitz family near the present-day Scotia Square Mall in Halifax. Afraid that the Russian revolutionaries would disrupt their country's war effort, Canadian naval authorities detained Trotsky at Citadel Hill and briefly at a POW camp in Amherst. Held a few weeks illegally before being released, Trotsky was quickly courted by Lenin, joined the Bolshevik Party, and became the general in charge of the October Revolution in Lenin's absence.[27]

Clearly, in the words of Harry Chapman, the Starr company "had brought Dartmouth international recognition with the manufacture of the spring skate, which revolutionized ice hockey and skating. Modern-day hockey and ice-skating trace their origin to the skates made at the Dartmouth plant."[28]

Halifax Regional Municipality purchased the Starr property in November 1996 to include it in development plans for a park along the Shubenacadie Canal. It was hoped that the 1860 turbine system would be preserved, with a portion of the site being used for residential or commercial purposes. Unfortunately, during the debate as to its future use, a fire—apparently deliberately set—in the most historic section of the plant caused over $150,000 in damage.[29]

Although I grew up very close to the plant and walked by it on many occasions on the way to my law office in downtown Dartmouth, I had never been inside the factory. I was, however, fortunate to have been one of the very last persons to visit the plant in August 2000. Walking into the older section was like

Starr Manufacturing Limited, Dartmouth, Nova Scotia, circa 1890

walking 150 years back in time. The leather belts that operated the machinery from the water turbine still hung from the large beams in the open ceiling. Old equipment was scattered throughout the large, open work area. The turbine and sluice way that connected the factory to its water source from the Shubenacadie Canal were still visible in the basement. As I walked out of the old building, saddened by the damage caused by the fire and aware of its certain fate, I looked up to see an old horseshoe hanging on the plant's wall. But the Starr Factory's luck ran out: a few days later: the building was completely demolished—the loss of both a local and national treasure. In a dramatic and defiant display of its important heritage, the building surrendered a few boxes of unsold skates, apparently hidden in the basement, to the attacking bulldozers, having managed to hide them from prior inventories and a search and removal of historic items. A few lucky spectators were able to grab a significant souvenir from this sad day in our history. Anthony D. Barlow, architect and historic building consultant, completed an historical

assessment of the architecture of the Starr Building. In an essay entitled "Heritage Recording of the Starr Manufacturing Company Factory," Barlow concludes:

> There is no doubt that the Starr Manufacturing Company site was of national, if not international, significance. Inclined planes were constructed in North America and Europe to meet the commercial transportation needs of the Industrial Revolution. Water powered inclined planes such as the one constructed on the Morris and Shubenacadie canals are rare. Of the twenty- three powered inclined planes formerly employed on the Morris Canal, none of the aboveground superstructures of their powerhouses have survived. At Dartmouth, despite fire damage incurred in 1998, there still exists significant recognizable elements of the powerhouse. While the Shubenacadie Canal had a checkered history, it is an important symbol of Nova Scotian industrial and economic aspirations in the nineteenth century. As for Starr, the potential appeal of the Acme skate history was obvious in a country like Canada, which produces some of the finest ice hockey players and figure skaters in the world. Demolition of the property in 2000 represents a tragic loss.[30]

Although skate production stopped in 1939, the Starr plant continued operating until the mid-1990s.

Taken shortly before Starr's destruction, this photo shows the overhead wheels that transported power from the underground water turbine system to operate the plant's machinery.

Established in 1861, the Starr plant was used for the manufacture of nuts, bolts, hockey skates, sticks, and numerous iron items. During World War Two, the plant's workforce, eighty percent of which were women, produced artillery shells and rivets for the war effort. Although the building was demolished in 2000, the underground turbine and sluice that provided water power from the adjacent Shubenacadie Canal were preserved for possible future restoration.

This photograph was taken at the time of the destruction of the Starr Manufacturing Plant in August 2000. Note the large timber ship's knees, which were used to support the structure by bracing the outer beams. After conducting a historical survey of the property, Anthony D. Barlow described the support structure as "a striking example of maritime building techniques in an industrial setting."[31] Fortunately, some of these beams have been saved for possible use in reconstruction on the site.

PART IV

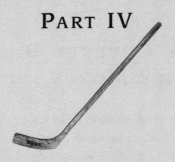

THE EVOLUTION
OF HOCKEY

In the 1860s indoor hockey rinks began to appear in Canada, with one of the earliest rinks being built in Halifax. Hockey would be able to take its next logical evolutionary step—the movement of the exciting game indoors. Other rinks would soon follow in both Halifax and Dartmouth and organized indoor leagues would flourish. To adapt to the indoor games, changes to the game of hockey would be required and the players from the area would once again provide many new innovations. Indoor games would allow for new teams and leagues, including mercantile teams, and leagues for women and Black players. Canada's game was rapidly growing from its Dartmouth and Halifax roots.

THE COVERED RINK—
HOCKEY MOVES INDOORS

Indoor skating rinks were first introduced in Canada in the early 1860s. One of the first covered ice rinks in Canada was erected at Horticultural Gardens in Halifax in 1863, just months after the Victoria Skating Rink was opened in Montreal. The pioneer skating rink was a wooden structure 180 x 60 feet, with an arched roof that was illuminated with coal gas. A reception room with a stove was located near the main entrance. A raised platform at the opposite end of the building was built to accommodate a band. On January 3, 1863, His Excellency the Earl of Mulgrave, Lieutenant-Governor of Nova Scotia, and his aides arrived to declare the rink open. The interior of the rink was decorated with flags and streamers. Following the opening ceremonies, which included the 17th Regiment band, sixty women in costume inaugurated the new rink with an exhibition of fancy skating.[1] Dr. Martin notes that organized games played in the new rink in the winter of 1863 were regularly reported in the local papers. "Hockey must have been a game of long standing in and about Halifax," he writes, "because the newspapers did not comment on anything extraordinary about the contests: which suggests that their readers were well acquainted with hockey procedure and practices. The only seeming novelty was that the game was played indoors for the first time, and necessarily limited the number of players on each side."[2]

With the introduction of artificial ice being more than thirty years away, natural ice was used in the rink; in the summer, the ice was floored for roller skating. The hockey goal stones were somewhat smaller than modern curling stones and were lined up parallel to the length of the rink about three or four feet apart, a carry-over from the first games of hockey played on our lakes. This rule was very sensible and practical—on the lakes and in the new rinks, which did not have boards surrounding the ice, the players wanted to discourage lifting the puck and promote stick handling rather than long shots on goal; without the benefit of protective gear, forwards and goaltenders wanted to protect themselves (and the spectators) from injury. A player therefore had to carry the puck to the opposite goal, and shoot sideways. Faced with this situation, the goalkeeper would defend the goal by placing one foot in front of the other, heel to toe, covering the remaining gap with his hockey stick.[3]

The period between the 1860s and the 1890s saw significant improvements to the goals. For goal posts, shoulder-high pieces of wood a bit thicker than a broom handle were placed in holes in the center of the stones. Three-sided goal boxes—like large packing boxes—about the same height as the goal posts followed. One objection to goal-boxes was that players were often body-checked against the sharp edges or the splintery sides of this "dangerous piece of architecture."[4] The introduction of the goal nets in 1899 was another first developed in Halifax and Dartmouth. A Halifax newspaper reported that the nets were first used in a game between the Crescents and the Wanderers on January 6, 1899. (In 1943, The Canadian Amateur Hockey Association incorrectly reported that nets were first introduced in 1900 in a game between the Montreal Shamrocks and Victorias.)[5]

Although an indoor rink would provide better protection from the cold and poor weather, the local press was quick to point out its shortfalls, observing in 1865:

> Griffin's Pond, on the Common, presented an animated scene last evening. Some two or three hundred of both sexes were congregated on the ice, the latter being in pretty good condition for skating: and to enhance the enjoyment of the occasion the moon beamed forth in all its splendor. Talk about Rinks! No inside exhibition— tame as it necessarily must be—could come up to the glorious skating in the open air last evening.[6]

Halifax's second rink, The Empire Rink Exhibition Building, was erected circa 1877 in Halifax on College Street, where the Cathedral Church of All Saints now

Halifax's second rink, the Exhibition Building, was a popular location for hockey games in the 1880s. Without boards surrounding the ice surface, rules were developed with the protection of spectators and players in mind. Goal posts, for example, were turned sideways to discourage long shots on the goal.

stands. Eventually, larger rinks were built, including the Halifax Forum and the Pepperell Street arena. The Empire Rink played an important role in the development and caliber of play of the Wanderers' Hockey Club of Halifax. The Wanderers would subsequently defeat the previously dominant Dartmouth Chebuctos for the coveted Starr Manufacturing trophy in 1897.[7]

In the 1880s, the Dartmouth Agricultural Society decided to build a new exhibition building in Dartmouth on lands forming part of the common—the subsequent location of Park School. In a drive for funds, Chairman George J. Troop and his committee sold $3,500 worth of shares for a long, two-storey galleried structure with cattle sheds lining the rear yard. Built entirely of spruce, the rink's dimensions were 190 x 50 feet with an ice oval of 175 x 50 feet. The rink building was designed by architect Henry Elliot, who in 1868 built a farmhouse in Dartmouth to provide his large family with a rural atmosphere. The farmhouse later became the first Brightwood Golf Club clubhouse.[8]

Used each winter as a rink, the Dartmouth Exhibition Building was home of the Dartmouth Chebuctos—winners of every game played in the Maritimes from 1887 to 1894. The lighthouse was constructed in 1907 and was cared for by William Patterson, who was also the ice maker. The second Park School was built on the site in 1918 after the Halifax Explosion destroyed the exhibition building.

In *Like a Weaver's Shuttle*, Joan and Lewis Payzant report that this excellent skating rink was in operation in Dartmouth by 1885. There, two or three carnivals were held each winter at which a band played to revelers dressed in unique and original costumes:

> The band of the 66th Princess Louise Fusiliers travelled from Halifax
> to provide music for the skaters, and the bandsmen were granted a

rare privilege: they were allowed a return trip on the boats for the price of a single fare. On band days admission to the rink was 15 cents, on ordinary days ten cents. Tickets were on sale in Halifax at the Steam Boat Company's office only, and these tickets included ferriage. The secretary of the rink was A.C. Johnston, son of director J.W. Johnston of the Steam Boat Company.[9]

In the early days of indoor hockey games, players often engaged in races between periods or after the game. Halifax and Dartmouth had some of the finest speed skaters in North America.

On Saturdays, the ice would often be booked in the morning for youth hockey league games, in the afternoon for fancy skating to the tunes of an orchestra, and in the evening for match games among the various firms of Halifax and Dartmouth. The newspapers even carried paid announcements by firms challenging other "mercantile hockey teams" to hockey matches:

> William Stairs Son and Morrow's hockey team challenges any mercantile hockey team in the city to a friendly game of hockey, date and other particulars to be arranged. Employees of Clayton and Sons preferred. (Signed) W.H. Fraser, Manager.[10]

Every team had enthusiastic supporters and rooters who sometimes marched in procession up from the ferry waving their flags and banners. The wooden, galleried rink soon became a "nightly mecca" in winter for all Dartmouthians, with hockey as the main attraction. The rink became the home of the Chebucto Amateur Athletic Club, the Maritime hockey champions from 1887 to 1894. It was especially busy when the Halifax Wanderers or Crescents teams played the Chebuctos, the Knockabouts, or the Mutuals of Dartmouth. In 1896, a Dartmouth newspaper printed the following words about hockey in the area:

For years past the Dartmouth Lakes have been the scene of thousands of games of "shinney" in which any number of players participated. The game in ye olden times was generally played with a stone for a puck, and hockey sticks rudely fashioned from roots of trees. Now things are different.

About ten years ago the Chebucto team organized. They were mere boys gathered together on occasion to play the Halifax Wanderers. From that day to this, a Dartmouth team has been defeated only once by a City team.

For many years the Chebuctos alone supported this now highly popular game. It was then played in the old-fashioned way. A wooden puck. No lifting. And the goals composed of two stones, placed in opposite position to what they are now.[11]

Dr. Martin notes that Dartmouth's hockey players developed to the point where the Dartmouth Chebuctos competed for the equivalent of the Stanley Cup in 1889. He wrote:

Seven men played continuously for two 30-minute periods, unless injured. The hockey sticks had broad blades with handles rounded like a broom. The puck was an oblong-shaped block of lignum vitae wood. The goals were similar to curling stones placed parallel with the length of the rink to prevent goals being scored by lifting. The Chebucto team went to Montreal and played two games for what was equivalent to the Stanley Cup, on Feb. 25 and 27, 1889. One half-period was played under Canadian Hockey Association rules and the other half under Halifax rules. The Chebuctos lost both games.[12]

A significant contribution of the Chebuctos was the introduction of the forward pass to the game in Montreal. It is interesting to note as well that Charles Patterson, great-uncle of popular Dartmouth journalist Arnie Patterson, competed in an exhibition skating race with Charles Gordon, one of the fastest skaters in Montreal, who was the eventual victor in the three-mile race.[13]

Further information concerning the rules of hockey were given by Dr. Martin in an article written in 1955 entitled "Hockey in the Old Days." Seven men always constituted a hockey team and the defence men were known as the "point" and "cover-point." The teams would play two thirty minute periods with a five or ten minute break. Up to the first few years of the 1890s, the puck which was used was an oblong block of hard, heavy wood known as "lignum vitae." For night hockey on the lakes or harbour, the puck of choice was a battered tin-can "for audible reasons in the inky darkness." At the first rink games in Halifax, a solid rubber ball was used.[14]

Although the fortunes of the Chebuctos lessened in the 1890s, their junior team won their 110th game without a defeat—perhaps a record for any league.

The tradition of company teams and matches, which started in Dartmouth and Halifax in the 1880s, continued to be popular into the 1900s. The Halifax Post Office Hockey Team, 1909, (top) features J.T. (Jim) Martin (brother of Frank, Dee and John), and the M.T.& T. Company team (bottom) features W.A. (Dee) Martin.

Their line-up consisted of Robert Cameron in goal; Fred Granger, point; Austin Kane, cover point; Ernest Lahey, left wing; Jack Allen, right wing; George Young, rover and Captain Harry "Nig" Young, centre. The team was so popular that a poem was printed in the *Atlantic Weekly* praising the efforts:

> Oh "Nig" you are a dandy,
> And Lahey's just the same;
> Granger, he's a good one,
> And plays a roarin' game.
>
> Cameron as a goal man,
> He simply can't be beat;
> A cyclone couldn't stop him,
> Or knock him off his feet.[15]

Dr. Martin concludes his hockey references with an interesting summary of the development of the sport:

> The advent of rubber heels put an end to the practice of boring a gimlet-hole into the centre of leather heels so as to fasten the boot to the old-type wooden skate. When the boots were in ordinary use, the hole was plugged with a slim cylinder of paper. The practice had been partly abandoned with the invention of the Acme spring skates in the 1860s. At the turn of the century, however, it went out almost completely when there was designed a brand new style of skate to be affixed permanently to a special skating boot, better known as a hockey-boot.
>
> This improvement gave a decided impetus to the speeding-up of ice hockey because it greatly lessened the number of delays which had hitherto resulted from the unreliable method of clamping spring-skates to ordinary street boots. The Starr Manufacturing Company led, or kept pace with the various changes, and were continually experimenting with metal skates of different degrees of toughness. They encouraged amateur hockey by donating a large silver trophy which for many seasons was emblematic of the Maritime Hockey Championship.
>
> After the Chebucto hockey team returned from Montreal, they introduced some Upper Canadian customs hereabouts. For instance the lignum vitae block of wood disappeared, and the modern flat rubber puck bounced into the game. Early in the 1890's, they rearranged the goal-stones so as to be at right-angles to the length of the rink, which move made possible the scoring of goals by lifting. Occasionally the opposing defence men would exchange two or three long lifts in slow succession, giving the others the only respite

in their grueling grind, for there was no such thing as a change of players. Seven men went on the ice for two half-hour periods, and stayed there. If a player suffered injury, the opposing side generally, not always, dropped one of their men.

Some Halifax and Dartmouth hockeyists were very adept at the art of lifting, and could vault the puck high over the hanging lights to land it dead-on the distant goal, although they often overshot the mark and hit spectators in the gallery. These high lifts were executed, in the case of a right-hand man, by the player making a right turn and bringing down the slanting blade of his stick sharply against the lower rim of the puck.[16]

The Chebucto Amateur Athletic hockey team, 1887-1888, from left to right, (front) George Pyke and Frank Young; (middle) John Brown, Judson Hyde, John A. Young; (back) H.D. Creighton, Walter Faulkner, Charles Patterson, Charles Robson. In 1889, the team of Dartmouth players competed in Montreal for the equivalent of the Stanley Cup. Unfortunately, the team lost both games.

In 1896, the Halifax Hockey Association was formed, with the Chebuctos, Ramblers, Crescents, Wanderers, and Dalhousie clubs as members. For the first time in a decade, the Dartmouth Chebuctos almost lost their championship honours, but defeated the Crescents in the final game. In 1897, the Mutuals and United

The Halifax Crescents were the 1898 champions of the Halifax Hockey League. The team proudly displays the Starr Manufacturing Trophy, which was donated by the company in 1897.

Banks replaced Dalhousie and the Ramblers in the fight for the "magnificent trophy" donated by the Starr Manufacturing Company, which was won by the Wanderers in a play-off, with a score of three to one. In 1898, the Crescents would win the season without a single loss, and in 1899 they took the Starr trophy.[17] On February 8, 1900, The *Halifax Herald* reported on a game between the Crescents and the Chebuctos in which the Crescents proved their skill:

> The Hockey game at the north-end rink last night between the Crescents and Chebuctos was a very one-sided affair. The former team was victorious by a score of ten goals to nothing. The Chebuctos played for ten minutes but after that they took little interest in the game. The team, too, was weakened by the absence of Gates at point. Considerable delay was caused in the first half by the playing of the puck before the whistle blew. In the second half, two men were put off the ice for handling the puck too early. Several other men were sent to the Boards for tripping.[18]

THE GAME OF HOCKEY
TRAVELS WESTWARD

Having become well established both outdoors and indoors in Dartmouth and Halifax, the game of hockey began to spread across Canada. In the 1870s, hockey was introduced to Montreal by J.G.A. Creighton of Halifax, who suggested to his friends and fellow Victoria Skating Club members that they obtain sticks from Halifax and start playing the game. Creighton had become a member of the club in 1874 after being nominated as a figure skating judge by his former Halifax club. On March 3, 1875, two teams of friends from the Montreal club played hockey at the Victoria Skating Rink according to "Halifax Rules."[19] *The Montreal Gazette* announced the game on the day it was played, and ran an article about it the next day in which it was noted that "hockey, though much in vogue on the ice in New England and other parts of the United States, is not known much here."[20] Although this statement might suggest that hockey had started in New England, in 1859, *The Boston Evening Gazette* reported that ricket or hockey—"the most exciting game displayed on the ice"—was Nova Scotia's favourite pastime. The editors emphasized that the game would be "a fine addition to our winter sports" and, in fact, "sent down for a set of hurleys preparatory to its introduction."[21]

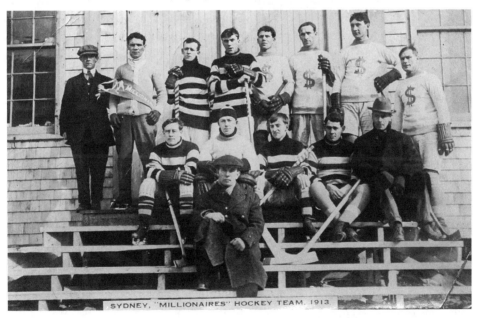

SYDNEY, "MILLIONAIRES" HOCKEY TEAM. 1913

This postcard of the Sydney "Millionaires" team, addressed to "Frank Martin, Liverpool, N.S,"
reads: "Say Frank, this is some hockey team. I saw them play Moncton last Thursday—Cliff."
Clifford Smith played hockey with Frank on a 1909 Dartmouth team.

Hockey enthusiast William Reynolds Harris, circa 1900.

Speed skaters Charles and Alexander Patterson with their medals and Starr racing skates, in 1891. Charles was a member of the famous Dartmouth Chebucto hockey team.

In 1877, an article in the McGill University Gazette contained a notice for a meeting to form a university hockey club, noting that a few members had played on January 21, 1877. The McGill club played against the Montreal club, of which Creighton was the captain, in 1877. By this time, Montreal is credited with having devised their own rules for the game, apparently by simply adopting the field hockey rules created in England in 1875 (see Appendix A). Unlike their Halifax counterparts, who played with seven players and invented the term "rover" for the seventh man, the Montrealers used nine players on each side and did not allow forward passes. All players were required to remain onside and the game concluded after three goals were scored by the winning team. The goalie was required to remain standing at all times.[22]

Hockey would continue to spread to other areas of Canada, and, by the beginning of the 1900s, a fixed set of rules was being applied throughout most of the country. In 1905, the Dartmouth Hockey League Schedule of Games contained the Laws of Hockey (see Appendix B), which were identical to the rules adopted by the Halifax League two years earlier with one important exception—Dartmouth included specifications for the goals while their Halifax neighbors provided that the regulation goal net adopted by the Canadian Hockey Association would prevail. Reviewing these rules confirms an important fact—the game of hockey has continued to evolve; it is clear that even in the early 1900s, the game was significantly different than it is today.[23]

J.G.A. CREIGHTON

Born in Halifax on June 12, 1850, Creighton was educated at the Halifax Grammar School, Dalhousie University, and McGill University. After completing his bachelor of arts degree in 1868 at Dalhousie, he was employed by various companies, including the Lachine Canal Company, until 1877. Creighton obtained his bachelor of civil law in 1880, and two years later was appointed law clerk of the Senate, a position he held for forty-eight years until his death in 1930.[24] Based on an interview with Henry Joseph, a member of McGill's first hockey team, the following article appeared in the *Montreal Gazette* in 1936:

J.G.A. Creighton, 1850–1930

> Mr. Joseph, who is a graduate of McGill, recalls that a student friend, J.C.A. Creighton was responsible for the start of hockey here (in Montreal). Skating was popular in the city, and most of the enthusiasts belonged to the Victoria skating club, with their headquarters in the old Victoria Rink, which was built around the year 1860 [1862]. It was Creighton who first suggested that they obtain hockey sticks from Halifax and take up the game. Creighton, a McGill Student, came from Halifax, and had seen the game played in his home town, which is sufficient proof that if the Maritime centre is not the actual home of ice hockey, it at least predates the birth of the game here. The suggestion of Creighton was taken up and several clubs began playing friendly games here.[25]

Creighton never claimed the title "father of hockey." In 1926, however, he did claim "the honour of being captain of the first regular hockey club to be formed in Montreal in 1877."[26] Being from Halifax, where hockey had been played regularly for many years, Creighton seems to have recognized that his primary contribution to the sport was as captain of the first regular hockey club to be formed not in the country, but, as he says, in Montreal.

A CRACK AT THE CUP

After winning eight straight games in 1900, the Crescents were poised for a greater challenge: to compete for the Stanley Cup. The gold-lined silver bowl known as the Stanley Cup was donated in 1892 by Lord Frederick Arthur Stanley, governor-general of Canada from 1888 to 1893, to be awarded yearly to the amateur hockey champions of Canada. On February 10, 1900, *The Halifax Herald* reported: "The Stanley Cup challenge by the Crescents to the Shamrocks of Montreal has not yet been answered. The date for the game will be arranged in March."[27] On February 20, 1900, *The Halifax Herald* would once again report on the upcoming challenge:

> Montreal—The Shamrock Hockey club will have lots of hard work during the next three weeks. While they are pleased to have the opportunity of playing the Crescents of Halifax for the Stanley Cup, they are not pleased that the dates mentioned, come right in on their recent programme and as the challenge of the Crescents will certainly be accepted, it means a very busy time for the Shamrocks. At present they are scheduled for matches on Feb. 27, March 3 and 8 and have promised to play a match in Quebec on the tenth. The dates mentioned by the Crescents, March 5, 7 and 9 it will be seen, interfere somewhat with those arrangements, and if carried out will mean hard work for the Shamrocks. The Shamrocks have not yet heard from the trustees of the Stanley Cup in regard to the Crescents' challenge.[28]

On February 27, 1900, the newspapers reported that the Halifax Crescents were preparing for their big challenge to the Montreal Shamrocks. The following article appeared under the headline "Halifax Champions Defeat the New Yorkers in International Hockey Contest at North Rink":

> The international match last night between the Crescents and All New York team resulted in a victory for the Crescents 12 to 3. The ice was in perfect condition (natural) and lots of combination work could be indulged in. The play was fast from start to finish—the Crescents scoring 6 in the first half, with another 6 in the second. The New York team played good hockey, and expect to make a better showing tonight.
>
> Kane, (point) for the Crescents played a star game, allowing very few to get past him. Maher's rushes and tackles meant a lot for his team. Crockett played a swift game and Bishop's goal-keeping was

stonewall. Mr. Fitzpatrick refereed and gave satisfaction. 1,500 people enjoyed the game.[29]

"On the following day," notes Halifax sports writer Hugh Conrod, "the press apparently forgot to cover the match—or it simply wasn't used, as there was no account of the second game. However, there was an advertisement for Mic Mac Hockey stick 'trade mark copyrighted,' of the highest quality and most approved pattern, by the Starr Manufacturing Co. Ltd. of Dartmouth, who also manufactured the world's most popular brand of Acme skates at the time."[30]

The Halifax Herald reported the results of the Stanley Cup challenge on March 6, 1900:

> Shamrocks 10—Crescents 2 Champions Excelled the Halifax Men as Stick Handlers and in Team Work.
>
> Montreal—March 5—The world champion Shamrocks again demonstrated here tonight their prowess as the greatest of hockey players at the present time. They defeated the Halifax Crescents 10 goals to 2. Nearly 3,000 spectators enjoyed the novel exhibition from start to finish. The experienced Shamrocks never appeared anything but absolutely sure winners. The half time read Shamrocks 6, Crescents 1. The Crescents proved to be a fine lot of skaters having a little difficulty keeping on the puck when in Shamrocks possession. (Crescents had Bishop in goal; Kane on point; Mullane on Cover Point; and forwards—Mahar, Crockett, Ryan and McInnis.)

Unfortunately, the Halifax team did not have better luck in the second game:

> Shamrocks 11—Crescents 0 A Fast and Furious Game—Three Points of Weakness in Halifax Team.
>
> Montreal—March 8—The Shamrocks decisively vanquished the Stanley Cup challengers from Halifax—the Crescents, tonight by 11 straight goals. The Shamrocks tallied seven goals in the first half, on good straight hockey, and though Crockett and Ryan kept well on the puck, checking and breaking through with plucky tenacity, the local forwards were too clever. On the 6th and 7th goals, Mullane, Kane and Bishop's stubborn defence irritated Trihey and Brannen. Trihey slugged Mullane over the arms and was ruled off and repeatedly warned. Kane piled Brannen up in the corners. Besides blocking and stopping everything in sight, Kane's work was most effective. In the second half, referee Baird let everything go. Brannen was tripped and slashed Crockett and was warned. Trihey socked Mullane and Ryan good and hard. The Crescents showed pluck and stamina but inexperience, poor team play and wretched shooting lost for the Crescents. It was rough generally with the

Crescents reciprocating in equal measure. The Crescents leave Montreal Thursday night.[31]

As the new century began, an intense rivalry was developing between the Dartmouth and Halifax teams. In 1905, Dartmouth teams would create their own hockey league after disputes with their neighbors over gate receipts and complaints that the four Dartmouth teams were "practically ignored" by the league management in Halifax. The new league would feature the Centrals (represented by William "Dee" Martin), the Banooks (Frank Angwin and W.G. Foster), North Star (John Gavell) and the Woodside club (Alfred Gates and John Hogan). The 1905 Schedule of Games for the Dartmouth Hockey League confirms the reasons for the new league and, more importantly, offers a significant clue with respect to hockey's origin—twenty-five years before the first debate on hockey's birthplace:

Our Own Hockey League

The formation of an independent Hockey league is the best move that Dartmouth has made in connection with this sport since the original Chebucto team first took the field against all comers. Dartmouth did more for the introduction and establishment of hockey as a recognized athletic sport than any other town in the maritime provinces and could not submit to being gradually but surely crowded out of the field of which it was one of the first occupants. Long before this and while the city of Toronto was yet a forest, Dartmouth was playing lively hockey matches against the Indians on the lakes.

Halifax has never treated our town just right. When Dartmouth held the front rank in hockey the Wanderers dropped out of the game altogether and they have always shown more or less jealousy by acts such as forfeiting an important game with the Chebuctos in 1902 after pocketing heavy gate receipts from a previous game. In this connection it should be said that the decision of the Dartmouth league to pool the gate receipts and divide them, is a very wise one. This league will probably go a long way toward bringing Dartmouth back to its old enviable place in hockey.[32]

The intense rivalry or the unsuccessful attempt for the Stanley Cup would pale in comparison to an event that would strike Dartmouth and Halifax. On the morning of Thursday, December 6, 1917, during the First World War, a munitions ship named the *Mont Blanc* steamed up from the mouth of the harbour where it had been anchored the previous night. At the same time, the Norwegian steamer *Imo*, chartered for Belgian relief purposes, sailed out of Bedford Basin from the opposite direction. At the narrowest point of the harbour, the two ships collided. The resulting explosion from the *Mont Blanc's* cargo of TNT, tons of picric acid, and a deckload of benzol drums was the second-largest man-made explosion in history. Standing on the east side of Windmill Road on a hilltop without any sheltering houses in the vicinity, the Dartmouth rink was directly in the path of the terrific

The Halifax Explosion of 1917 destroyed much of Dartmouth and Halifax, including Dartmouth's only hockey rink.

concussion created by the explosion. With over 1600 deaths and the destruction of hundreds of buildings in the north ends of both towns, hockey and other winter pastimes naturally received little attention that winter.[33]

In 1923, a new arena was built in Dartmouth near the northeast corner of School Street and Wyse Road at a cost of $44,000. The Marks-Cross Arena was a steel-framed wooden structure with a large ice surface. Almost 5000 spectators could be accommodated in the new arena. Unfortunately, fire destroyed the rink in 1933, but it would be replaced once again.[34] As a young boy, I remember playing in the last of the wooden Dartmouth rinks on Windmill Road, which was also destroyed by fire in 1974. Watching the many teenaged "rink rats," as they were

The Marks-Cross arena was constructed in Dartmouth in 1923 and could accommodate five thousand spectators.

This photo of the Dartmouth Amateur Athletic Association hockey team in the early 1900s shows the players wearing their Starr skates.

Dartmouth Squirts, 1971. The photo was taken in the last wooden arena in Dartmouth, which was destroyed by fire in 1974. I am third from the right in the back row, wearing hockey pants that belonged to my grandfather.

known, cleaning the ice with hand plows and large portable watering tanks is a vision that often passes through my mind as I watch the electric Zamboni quickly circle the rinks at today's games.

WOMEN'S HOCKEY

With the first women's world hockey championship being held in 1990 and the introduction of the sport to the Olympics for the first time in 1994, the participation of women in hockey would appear to be a recent phenomenon. However, women have been skating, in Halifax and Dartmouth at least, since the mid-1800s, and they began playing hockey in organized leagues by the 1890s.[35] Their participation in these sports was of course hampered by Victorian standards of propriety, not to mention Victorian dress. In 1865, *The Acadian Recorder* published an article from a Connecticut newspaper questioning whether women should be skating at all:

OUGHT LADIES TO SKATE?

The practice of skating by females cannot be denounced in too strong terms; their formation forbids such violent and peculiar motion. I should as soon think of permitting a daughter to play base ball for exercise. The evil consequences to young ladies, resulting from the practice of skating, are beginning to be realized. We are informed that nearly every physician can bear testimony against the amusement as far as they are concerned. There are only occasional deaths by drowning; but it is now believed that where one life is lost in this way, there are hundreds of females whose sickness and death could be traced to the effects of skating. The practice of putting skates upon children in our parlors, is equally injurious and therefore cruel. I cannot believe that any lady in our town would ever again put on skates, were she aware of the injury to which she is liable in consequence. As so many proofs can be given against this exercise by females, I hope the time is not far distant when this masculine amusement will be abandoned by our young ladies.[36]

But as skating gained in popularity, women evidently would not be left out. Dr. Martin attributes women's willingness in the 1860s to participate in skating to "the simplicity of the Starr spring skates." He remarks that "they evidently had not practised [the pastime of skating] very extensively up to that time."[37] A newspaper article from 1866 supports Dr. Martin's conclusion:

Yesterday the tug 'Neptune' cut a channel and ferried people over at 3 cents a head. The enterprise was well rewarded. The last time the harbor was frozen over, was some six years ago. Then there was not a young lady to be seen skating on the surface, as this amusement had not yet become fashionable among the fair sex. Yesterday afternoon, however, there were perhaps as many as a hundred lady skaters on the harbor, and the gay dresses rendered the scene quite a colorful one. From Halifax on Friday night, parties could be seen walking across the ice to Dartmouth holding torchlights which reflected the light a great distance. Landing on the Dartmouth side, they appeared as if coming up out of the sea.[38]

In fact, when women began skating regularly, the local papers were quick to notice and remark on their proficiency, as the following article from The Halifax *Acadian Recorder* proves:

On Monday afternoon the ice on the ponds and lakes was in very fair condition for skating, the recent heavy falls of rain having effectually cleared away the snowy covering. The enclosed spots on the Common "literally groaned"—if such an expression may be used in connection with ice—beneath the weight of the hundreds who there did congregate, and who went whirling, sliding and sometimes tumbling over the surface in all directions. It was a subject of general remark that the "fair sex" mustered in strong force on this occasion and appearances would amply justify the belief that this amusement is in fact superseding all other winter recreations.

The young ladies of Halifax, too, are becoming rapid proficients in the art, and with a little assistance from one or more of the other sex at the first "go-of," in many instances mange ere long to outstrip their preceptors, causing the spectators to gaze with astonishment and admiration at the graceful sweeps and genteel curves and evolutions indulged in by the fair skaters.[39]

Miss Weir on Starr skates, circa 1880

In the early 1890s, hockey became a fast-growing sport among the women of Halifax and Dartmouth, and various women's teams competed in hockey games on a regular basis in the early years of the next century. There was an active women's hockey league in the Halifax area in 1913, featuring teams such as the Karanites (recognized by the 'K' on their sweaters) and the Halifax Red and Blue.[40] And women's hockey was catching on in other areas of the province as

Starr ad for ladies' hockey skates.

The Kananites Hockey Team, 1913, was one of many all-female hockey teams playing in Halifax and Dartmouth. Note the shin pads and interesting hats worn by the players.

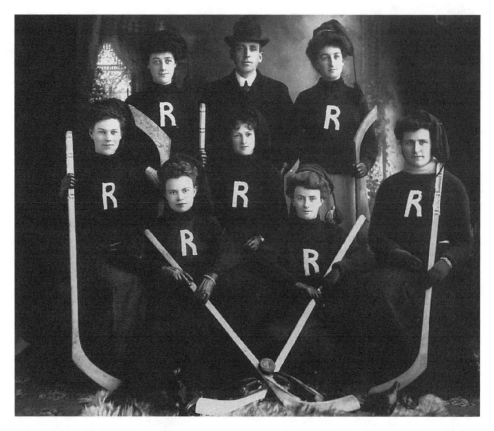

The Dartmouth Ramblers Women's Hockey Team—1907. (Back row, left to right): B. Colter, goal; H.A. Young, manager; R. Merson, point: M.Carter, rover: H.A. Young, captain, c.point; A. Hutchinson, centre; K. Patterson, right wing; and Miss Kane, left wing.

well. During the winter of 1911/1912, my grandfather, Frank J. Martin, moved to Liverpool, Nova Scotia, to assist with the organization of women's hockey there. Originally part of a group of Dartmouthians who were hired to perform a play and play a baseball game in Liverpool for Labour Day, he and friend Pip Griffin decided to stay for the winter to open a dry-cleaning business and assist with women's hockey. As explained in a later newspaper story, their stay made quite an impression:

> Besides stirring up the staid citizens of south shore Liverpool by the formation of a couple of girls hockey teams, the Dartmouth sportsmen Martin and Griffin got themselves involved in other humorous incidents, one of them the day they burned a big hole in the mayor's formal dress suit. News of the World Series baseball results had so distracted the ironer that the flat-iron went right through the material. It took the seamstress, Maude Peachsome anxious minutes with a needle to patch the damage without detection.[41]

My grandfather, Frank Martin (at left, middle row) and his fellow Liverpool champions.

Frank and Pip visited their friends at Ungar's Laundry in Halifax, where they picked up a pair of shoes that had been recovered from the S.S. *Titanic* after it sank on April 14, 1912. Halifax played a prominent role in the disaster, with many rescue ships arriving in the port after the tragedy to bury the deceased passengers. Coincidentally, Frank's brother, Dr. John Martin, happened to be working in the telegraph office on the night of the sinking and was involved in the receipt of early reports on the sinking. The *Titanic* shoes were displayed in the Liverpool dry-cleaning store window until Martin and Pip received a letter from prominent Halifax lawyer Robert Finn, a Dartmouth neighbour of the Martins, who advised that the shoes were the property of Isadore Strauss, a wealthy New Yorker who died in the tragedy.

AFRICAN NOVA SCOTIANS
TAKE UP THE GAME

National Hockey League superstar and 2002 Olympic gold medallist Jarome Iginla is one of only a few professional Black hockey players in a game traditionally dominated by white players. One might assume that the appearance of Black athletes in the game of hockey is only a recent occurrence, but at the beginning of the twentieth century, teams consisting entirely of Black players were common in the Halifax and Dartmouth area. In fact, these teams were playing at least as early as 1895. On February 23 of that year, *The Acadian Recorder* reported: "The match in the Dartmouth rink, Tuesday, between the Eurekas of Halifax and the Jubilees of Dartmouth, both colored teams, was very interesting. After a hard contest, which resulted in a draw, 1-1, it was decided to play a return match."[42] Three local teams participated in the Coloured Hockey League of the Maritimes, which was formed in 1900 and consisted of seven teams. The historic Black community of Africville in the north end of Halifax was represented by the Seasides. The Halifax Eurekas and the Dartmouth Jubilees also participated in the new league.

The Brown Bombers team displaying a number of its trophies. At the start of the twentieth century, numerous Black hockey teams existed in the Halifax and Dartmouth area.

To attract fans to the new leagues, the teams often performed acrobatics on the ice between periods. It was the acrobatics of Black goaltenders that led to a significant change in the traditional rules of hockey. Only in the Black leagues were goaltenders allowed to drop onto the ice to stop the puck. This significant hockey innovation soon became popular and was adopted by the N.H.L. in 1917.[43] Previously, goaltenders in that league had to stay on their skates when reaching for the puck.[44]

"The Champion Coloured Hockey Team, Halifax," circa 1910.

Hockey writer Joseph Romain remarked that the game of hockey did not exist as a sport until "some standards were met" in Montreal in the 1870s: "They are not the same standards we play today, but they are enough like them to recognize the game, and records have been kept of when, why, and by whom the standards were changed. This is the mark of a sport, as opposed to a folk game."[45] To suggest that the game played in Halifax and Dartmouth was a folk game is contrary to the facts that exist with respect to our extensive hockey heritage. Evidence shows that the game was played in a rink in Halifax and that rules, the Halifax rules which were transplanted to Montreal, were applied. Even if the game had not yet been played in a rink with written rules, was it no less a sport? Was baseball not a sport until it was played in a stadium? Was the game Wayne Gretzky played in his backyard with his family or the one that Paul Henderson played with frozen toes on a pond with friends not hockey? The Oxford Dictionary defines sport as a "game; outdoor pastime." What was played on our lakes was sport in its purest form—in Montreal, hockey took the first steps to becoming a sport business.

The available evidence clearly shows that hockey was in fact played outdoors in Halifax and Dartmouth for many years with goaltenders and on skates. While an article in *The Globe and Mail* of January 10, 2002, states that dozens and sometimes hundreds of players were playing the game, and that goaltenders were not used,[47] I did not find one reference during my research to suggest more than twenty players participated at any one time, and, quite clearly, the use of goal-

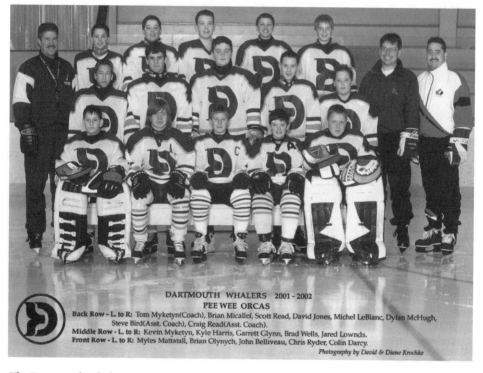

DARTMOUTH WHALERS 2001 - 2002
PEE WEE ORCAS
Back Row - L. to R: Tom Myketyn(Coach), Brian Micallef, Scott Read, David Jones, Michel LeBlanc, Dylan McHugh, Steve Bird(Asst. Coach), Craig Read(Asst. Coach).
Middle Row - L. to R: Kevin Myketyn, Kyle Harris, Garrett Glynn, Brad Wells, Jared Lownds.
Front Row - L. to R: Myles Mattatall, Brian Olynych, John Belliveau, Chris Ryder, Colin Darcy.
Photography by David & Diane Krochko

The Dartmouth Whaler's Minor Hockey Association's name and logo reflect another important period of our history. In 1775, sixteen Nantucket Quaker whaler families moved to Dartmouth to avoid British tariffs imposed on the newly independent United States. The families stayed only a few years before moving to Milford Haven, Wales, to build a new whaling industry. When the whaling colony was dismantled in 1791, twenty-two whaling ships were sailing out of Dartmouth.[46] The house that Quaker whaler William Ray built in 1788 is now a museum in downtown Dartmouth.

In 1994, the Dartmouth Whaler's organization adopted a Fair Play program designed to "enhance and foster SAFETY, RESPECT and FUN, and enhance the many positive aspects of minor hockey for players, parents, coaches, officials and others involved" (D.W.M.H.A. website). Many other associations have since adopted this successful program.

tenders was invented here. It is not a coincidence that the earliest written refer-ences to hockey on ice come from the Halifax newspapers. The skates and sticks that allowed the game to flourish and spread throughout Canada and the world were created here. The forward pass, goal nets, and goal keepers were invented in Halifax and Dartmouth. Hockey was first played indoors in the new rink in Halifax with smaller numbers of players.

With respect to the argument that evidence of written rules is required to sup-port the birthplace title, I refer to Dr. Fergusson's conclusions on this subject:

> ...let us turn for a moment to another important particular - drawing up of the first rules of the game....Investigators may agree that such a game was played in Montreal on that date, but they also believe that still earlier games were played in Kingston and Halifax, and they report that the first games in Montreal were played under what were then known as Halifax rules. This implies some sort of priority for Halifax....If Halifax rules were used in the so-called first game of 'true' ice hockey, which was played in Montreal in 1875, is it not rea-sonable to infer that those rules were evolved on ice, and not solely on paper, in Halifax?[48]

In fact, Montreal writer J.C. Beauchamp noted in 1940 that his research into the birthplace of hockey showed that "Halifax rules" and "Halifax Hockey club rules" were frequently recurring expressions. James W. Power, who wrote sports news and observations from the Maritimes to the *New York Spirit of the Times* be-ginning in 1879, provided important information concerning these rules:

> Anything previous to 1879 is not of my personal knowledge, the late James W. Power responded modestly, but Colonel Byron Arthur We-ston, then in his eighties,—now residing in Halifax, and a former res-ident of Dartmouth—who in his younger days was a prominent skater, tells me he played hockey in the sixties and that they had games with the MicMac Indians who resided near the lake. They played with a block of wood for a puck and the stones marking the place to score goals were placed at opposite angles to those at pres-ent. The main point of the rules were that there was to be no slash-ing, otherwise, not lifting the hockey stick above the shoulders and, when a goal was scored ends were changed. Players had to keep on-side and the forward pass was permitted.[49]

In *The Birthplace of Hockey* which was published in 1955, Dr. John Martin completed his article with the following plea:

> This concludes our summary of hockey history hereabouts. It has been compiled in these pages in the hope that the material will be preserved to provide some substantial evidence (not assumptions), that the Atlantic Provinces in general, and Dartmouth in particular, should get credit and recognition in any hockey Hall of Fame which

may be erected in Canada. The pioneer work of our ancestors in cradling and promoting outdoor hockey in our neighborhood, was a considerable contribution to the basis of the subsequent development of this popular winter pastime.[50]

There is no doubt that the game of hockey has evolved and changed for the better, and sometimes the worse, since its beginnings in our "City of Lakes." Significant changes were made to the game in the twentieth century: three twenty minute periods (1910), six players (1911), forward passes allowed between the blue lines (1918), passes within any of the three zones (1929-1930) and across blue lines (1930-31) and the introduction of the red line (1943-44).[51] The game today would look much different without the introduction of the slapshot by Boom Boom Geoffrion, Jacques Plante's goalie mask, Wayne Gretzky's domination of the game from behind the net, and the introduction of the red line and countless other rules made in the National Hockey League's head office in Montreal and subsequently New York. Did hockey as we know it not exist before any of these changes were initiated?

To suggest that the game of hockey which we know and love today did not start and evolve in Dartmouth and Halifax would be contrary to the historical

The historic Halifax Town Clock, built in 1803, is adjacent to the modern 10,000-seat Halifax Metro Centre. During the past twenty-five years, the Metro Centre has showcased numerous hockey teams, including the Calder Cup champion Nova Scotia Voyageurs, farm team to the Montreal Canadiens in the 1970s, and the Halifax Mooseheads, currently one of the most successful Major Junior teams in the country. The Metro Centre has hosted the World Figure Skating Championships and the Memorial Cup, and it will be the host arena for the 2003 IIHF World Junior Hockey Championship and the 2004 Women's World Hockey Championship.

facts that have been discovered to date. The suggestion that our area "lacked a stronger hockey bloodline than Montreal" is untenable.[52] Not only did our ancestors define the game on our many lakes and move it into the first indoor rinks, but they were the first to invent and produce the equipment and facilities which were essential for the game to flourish. The facts are clear—the first recorded games of hockey, the first hockey sticks and pucks, the modern skate which revolutionized skating and allowed the game to spread and be played on smaller rink ice surfaces, the birth of the forward pass, the use of goaltenders, the Halifax Rules, and the goal net all evolved in Halifax and Dartmouth.

When I play hockey with my children, David and Catherine, on our backyard rink, or watch Canada's Olympic teams fighting to win the gold medal, I feel a strong sense of pride for the great contribution we have made to Canada and the world of sport. And to think that it all started here in Dartmouth and Halifax—hockey's home!

Through the leadership of Dr. Edmund Morris and the financial support of Charles Keating, the Halifax Foundation placed numerous heritage markers throughout Dartmouth to celebrate its two-hundred-fiftieth anniversary. A block away from the Starr Manufacturing factory site, this marker proclaims Dartmouth the "Ice Skate Capital of the World." It is currently the only indication that the historic Starr plant existed in Dartmouth.

HOCKEY'S HOME

Downtown Halifax

Citadel Hill

Ferry

Starr Plant

Sullivan's Pond

Dartmouth

Shubenacadie
Canal Lock

Former Ice
Houses

Lake Banook

Dartmouth and Halifax's unique geography provided ideal conditions for the development of the game of ice hockey. This photo illustrates the close proximity of the various factors which played important roles in the development of the new sport. The soldiers of the Halifax Citadel and the sailors of the port were only a short ferry ride to Dartmouth's First Lake (Banook) and its perfect ice surface in winter months. The first lock of the Shubenacadie Canal entered Lake Banook from the adjacent Sullivan's Pond. One block from the pond was the most important skate factory in the world—the Starr Manufacturing Company. At Mi'kmaw encampments at nearby Tuft's Cove and on both Lake Banook and the adjacent Lake MicMac, the Mi'kmaq developed skills playing their own ice game and perfected the art of stick-making. With these perfect conditions, ice hockey was soon being played on Lake Banook and the North West Arm for the first time.

ENDNOTES

INTRODUCTION

1 *The Dartmouth Free Press*, January 28, 1981

2 Ibid.

3 Martin, "Birthplace"

4 Martin, *Dartmouth*, preface

5 *The Novascotian*, February 24, 1831

6 Fitsell, 159

7 SIHR Report, 16. In January, 2002, I had forwarded my preliminary research to the SIHR.

8 Ibid., 14

9 Ibid., 3, 15

10 Fitsell, 162

11 The Acme Skate was made by Dartmouth's Starr Manufacturing.

12 The "hot porter" apparatus carried porter, a dark brown bitter beer.

PART I

1 Saunders, 10.

2 Cassidy, 63.

3 Chapman, *Alderney*, 14–16, 26.

4 Martin, *Dartmouth*, 287.

5 Chapman, *Shubenacadie*, 2.

6 Ibid., 6-7, 10.

7 Martin, *Dartmouth*, 143-144.

8 Ibid., 177.

9 Ibid., 177.

10 In fact, Dr. Martin confused these terms by describing hurley as ground hockey. *Dartmouth*, 176.

11 *The Novascotian*, February 24, 1831, from Fergusson, "Early Hockey."

12 *Funk and Wagnalls Encyclopedia*, 4744.

13 Chapman, *Shubenacadie*, 31-41.

14 Martin, *Dartmouth*, 145.

15 Barlow, 202.

16 *The Novascotian*, January 22, 1829 from Beck, 107.

17 *The Acadian Reporter*, January 22, 1853.

18 Martin, "Hockey in the Old Days."

19 *The Halifax Reporter*, February 14, 1867.

20 Martin, *Dartmouth*, 217 and 563.

21 *The Evening Mail*, March 2, 1907, as reported in *The Chronicle-Herald*, March 9, 2002.

22 Martin, *Dartmouth*, 183.

23 Ibid., 284.

24 Ibid., 305.

25 Ibid., 363.

26 Ibid., 365.

27 Ibid., 381.

28 Ibid., 74.

29 Fergusson, 37.

30 Martin, *Dartmouth*, 562.

31 Chapman, *Alderney*, 31.

32 Payzant, 78.

33 Martin, *Dartmouth*, 464.

34 Bruce, 197 and Martin, *Dartmouth*, 464.

35 *The Halifax Reporter*, January 10 and 13, 1863.

36 Fingard, 117.

37 *The Acadian Recorder*, March 13, 1865.

38 *The Halifax Reporter*, January 24, 1863.

39 Ibid., January 27, 1863.

40 *The Acadian Recorder*, January 30, 1865.

PART II

1 Fergusson, 38.

2 Martin, "The Birthplace".

3 *Funk and Wagnalls Encyclopedia*, 4744.

4 *The Chronicle-Herald*, September 21, 1978.

5 *Chambers's*, 655.

6 SIHR, 6.

7 *Encarta Encyclopedia*—baseball.

8 Fitsell, "Windsor."

9 Windsor Heritage Hockey website. The extent of the controversy with respect to Windsor's birthplace claim is noted in a letter to the editor published in the Halifax *Chronicle-Herald* on January 10, 2002 (b2):

"WRONG POND

Dear Editor:

Re: your Jan. 4 front-page story titled "Windsor winds up for a shinny showdown."

In the photo caption, you state that Howard Dill stands on Long Pond. However, there is no proof that the pond on the Dill farm is actually "Long Pond." In fact, it was called "Steel Pond," a sulphur-spring-fed natural pond on the Dill farm. Long Pond, on the other hand, is an old, water-filled gypsum quarry on Sunny Slope Farm adjacent the Dill farm.

"Steel Pond" was enlarged by machinery to make it longer that it originally was. If it was a historical property, then why was it bulldozed to make it longer?

More hockey was probably played on Steel Pond that ever was played on Long Pond; but at the same time, this does not make it Long Pond. Certainly, this pond no longer looks anything like the original Dill farm pond.

What bothers me is that if someone with the proper credentials does not rectify this error or actually, by some twist of fate, declare the Dill Farm pond as the first place where hockey was played in Canada, for generations to come, people will be coming to the wrong location to pay homage to the Birthplace of Hockey.

As an "old boy" from KCS, I played pickup hockey on KCS Pond, Steel Pond and Long Pond. Now the names and locations have been changed or deleted—to satisfy what? Certainly not facts.

10 Cassidy, 204 and Eaton, 180–181.

11 Beck, v.2, 71.

12 Piers, 125-126.

13 Fergusson, 39.

14 Ibid., 39.

15 Ibid., 39.

16 Ibid., 38.

17 Ibid., 39.

18 Martin, "Birthplace."

19 Martin, *Dartmouth*, 343-344. In "The Babes in the

Woods," Dr. Martin advises that Mrs. Robert Gray, who grew up next to Lake Banook advised him that she watched hockey games on Banook in the 1850s.

20 Ibid., 351-352.
21 Fergusson, 41.
22 Ibid.,40.
23 Ibid.
24 Ibid.
25 SIHR, 15.
26 Martin, *Dartmouth*, 373.
27 Fitsell, 29.
28 Raddall, 281.

PART III

1 Martin, "Hockey."
2 Fitsell, 33.
3 Ibid., 59-60.
4 Dartmouth Heritage Museum, Starr Ad Collection, 1908.
5 Power, *The Halifax Mail*, March 23, 1943.
6 Ibid.
7 Hockey historian Bill Fitsell recently provided me with information on Dartmouth history that is probably known to very few of its citizens. He advised that a rock located on the shore of Lake MicMac (the second lake, adjacent to Lake Banook) is engraved with the name Cope, the year 1876, and an image of two schooners. A well-known Mi'kmaw family in the area, the Copes resided near the Dartmouth Lakes. Dr. Martin noted in *The Story of Dartmouth* (40) that they were prominent in the canoe races on the harbour and lakes and that, more significantly, Isaac Cope advised him that his family made many hockey sticks in the area where the rock is located.
8 Martin, *Dartmouth*, 40 and Chapman, *White Shirts*, 34.
9 Quinpool, 78.
10 *The Halifax Reporter*, January 6, 1863.
11 Martin, *Dartmouth*, 40.
12 *Chambers's*, 648.
13 Ibid. ,371.
14 *The Dalhousie Gazette*,1908 and *The Hamilton Herald*, 1909.
15 Martin, *Dartmouth*, 373.
16 Ibid., 41-42.
17 Ibid., 92.
18 Ibid., 390.
19 Ibid., 41 and 390 and Chapman, *White Shirts*, 37.
20 Chapman, *White Shirts*, 38.
21 Halifax Hockey League Schedule, 1903.
22 *Winnipeg Telegram*, November 12, 1908. (Starr ad collection).
23 Chapman, *Alderney*, 271-272.
24 Ibid. 312.
25 Trotsky, *My Life*, 4. I contacted the Bankfield Museum, Halifax, England, and was advised by June Hill that she had no knowledge of ice skates being produced there.
26 Halifax League Schedule, 1903.
27 Nunn, 135-136.
28 Chapman, *Alderney*, 488.
29 Ibid. 488-490.
30 Barlow, 213-214.
31 Barlow, 204

PART IV

1 Quinpool, 83.
2 Martin, "Birthplace."
3 Martin, "Hockey."
4 Ibid.
5 Power, *Halifax Mail*, March 23, 1943.
6 *Acadian Recorder*, January 13, 1865.
7 Martin, "Hockey."
8 Martin, *Dartmouth*, 62-63.
9 Payzant, 92.
10 Conrod, "Stanley Cup."
11 Martin, "Hockey" and Martin, *Dartmouth*, 459.
12 Martin, *Dartmouth*, 428.
13 Fitsell, 67.
14 Martin, "Hockey."
15 Martin, *Dartmouth*, 464 and 476–477.
16 Ibid.
17 Dartmouth Hockey League, 1905 and Halifax League Schedule
18 Conrod, "Stanley Cup."
19 Fergusson, 41-42.
20 SIHR, 10.
21 Fergusson, 39.
22 Fitsell, 34, 162.
23 Dartmouth Hockey League, 1905 and Halifax League Schedule
24 Fergusson, 41–42.
25 Menke, 1943.
26 Fitsell, 31.
27 Conrod, "Stanley Cup."
28 Ibid.
29 Ibid.
30 Ibid.
31 Ibid.
32 Dartmouth Hockey League
33 Martin, *Dartmouth*, 62-64.
34 Ibid., 69.
35 Nova Scotia Sport Hall of Fame
36 *The Acadian Recorder*, March 1, 1865.
37 Martin, *Dartmouth*, 371.
38 Ibid., 372.
39 *Acadian Recorder*, January 11, 1865.
40 Parker, 65.
41 *The Mail-Star*, May 5, 1978.
42 Menke, 15.
43 Nunn, *The Mail-Star*, Black Cultural Centre Collection.
44 Further research is required on Black and women's teams in Nova Scotia—two important hockey stories.
45 Romain, 7.
46 Martin, *Dartmouth*, 355.
47 S3
48 Fergusson, 38.
49 Power.
50 Martin, "Birthplace."
51 *Canadian Encyclopedia*, 1089.
52 Fitsell, 162.
53 Ibid., 34

BIBLIOGRAPHY

Akins, Thomas B. "History of Halifax City." *Nova Scotia Historical Society*. Vol VIII (1895).

Barlow, Anthony D. "Heritage Recording of the Starr Manufacturing Company Factory." *Industry and Society in Nova Scotia: An Illustrated History*, James E. Candow ed. Halifax: Fernwood Publishing, 2001.

Beck, J. Murray. *Joseph Howe Conservative Reformer 1804-1818*. Kingston and Montreal: McGill-Queen's University Press, 1984.

Bruce, Harry. *An Illustrated History of Nova Scotia*. Halifax: Nimbus Publishing Limited and Communications Nova Scotia, 1977.

Cassidy, Ivan. *Nova Scotia: All About Us*. Scarborough: Nelson Canada, 1983.

Chambers, Walter. *Chambers's Information for the People*. Edinburgh: W. & R. Charles, 1848.

Chapman, Harry. *In the Wake of the Alderney: Dartmouth, Nova Scotia, 1750-2000*. Dartmouth: Dartmouth Historical Association, 2000.

——————. *Men...Money and Muscle—Building the Shubenacadie Canal*. Dartmouth: The Dartmouth Historical Association, 1994.

——————. *White Shirts With Blue Collars: Industry in Dartmouth, Nova Scotia 1785-1995*. Dartmouth: Dartmouth Historical Association, 1997.

The Dartmouth Whalers Minor Hockey Association. www.whalers.org. July 2000.

Eaton, Arthur. *The History of Kings County*. Belleville, Ontario: 1972 (reprint of 1910 edition).

Fergusson, Dr. Bruce. "Early Hockey at Halifax." *Journal of Education for Nova Scotia*. 14: 4 June, (1965).

Fingard, Judith et al. *Halifax: The First 250 Years*. *Halifax*: Formac Publishing, 1999.

Fitsell, J.W. (Bill). *Hockey's Captains, Colonels & Kings*. Erin, Ontario: The Boston Mills Press, 1987.

——————. "Windsor, Nova Scotia: The Birthplace of Hockey?" *Society of International Hockey Research Journal*. December (1994).

Henderson, Paul. *Shooting for Glory*. Toronto: Warwick Publishing Inc., 1997.

Lawson, Mary. *History of the Townships of Dartmouth, Preston and Lawrencetown*. Halifax: Morton & Co., 1893.

Martin, Dr. John P. "The Birthplace of Hockey." Dartmouth: privately published, 1955.

——————. The Story of Dartmouth. Dartmouth: privately published, 1957.

——————. "Hockey in the Old Days." Dartmouth: privately published, 1955.

——————. "Babes in the Woods." Dartmouth: privately published, 1944.

Mintz, Patty. *Rediscover the Evangeline Trail*. Halifax: Nimbus Publishing Limited, 1996.

Menke, Frank K. *The New Encyclopedia of Sports*. New York: A.S. Barnes & Co., 1944.

—————. "The History of Hockey." *The Atlantic Sportsman*, 1948.

Nunn, Bruce. *History With a Twist*. Halifax: Nimbus Publishing Limited, 1998.

Patterson, Arnie. *Arnie Patterson: A Nova Scotian's Memoir*. Halifax: Nimbus Publishing Limited, 2001.

Payzant, Joan and Lewis. *Like A Weaver's Shuttle: A History of the Halifax-Dartmouth Ferries*. Halifax: Nimbus Publishing Limited, 1979.

Piers, Harry. "Artists in Nova Scotia." *Nova Scotia Historical Society*. 18 (1914).

Quinpool, John. *First Things in Acadia*. Halifax: First Things Publishers Limited, 1936.

Raddall, Thomas. *Halifax: Warden of the North*. London: J.M. Dent and Sons, 1948.

Romain, Joseph. *The Pictorial History of Hockey*. Greenwich: Brompton Books Corp., 1995.

Saunders, Gary L. *Discover Nova Scotia: The Ultimate Nature Guide*. Halifax: The Nova Scotia Museum and Nimbus Publishing Limited, 2001.

"Schedule and Rules of the Halifax Hockey League 1903."

"Schedule of Games—Dartmouth Hockey League 1905."

Society for International Hockey Research (SIHR). "Looking into the Claim that Windsor, N.S. is the birthplace of Hockey," May 2002.

Trotsky, Leon. *My Life (1930)*. Rev. ed. New York: Grosset & Dunlap, 1960.

The Windsor Hockey Heritage Society. <www.cnet.windsor.ns.ca/Pages/Hockey/home.html>

NEWSPAPERS:

Acadian Recorder, Halifax.

The Chronicle-Herald, Halifax.

Dartmouth Free Press, Dartmouth.

The Daily News, Halifax.

Dalhousie Gazette, Halifax.

The Globe and Mail, Toronto.

The Halifax Reporter, Halifax.

Halifax Mail, Halifax.

Hamilton Herald, Hamilton.

The Mail-Star, Halifax.

The Novascotian, Halifax.

APPENDIX A

PLAYING RULES

FOR THE

GAME OF HOCKEY.

1.—The game shall be commenced, and renewed by a Bully in the centre of the ground. Goals shall be changed after each game.

2.—When a player hits the ball, any one of the same side who at such moment of hitting is nearer to the opponents' goal line is out of play, and may not touch the ball himself, or in any way whatever prevent any other player from doing so, until the ball has been played. A player must always be on his own side of the ball.

3—The ball may be stopped, but not carried or knocked on by any part of the body. No player shall raise his stick above his shoulder. Charging from behind, tripping, collaring, kicking or shinning shall not be allowed.

4.—When the ball is hit behind the goal line by the attacking side, it shall be brought out straight 15 yards, and started again by a Bully; but, if hit behind by any one of the side whose goal line it is, a player of the opposite side shall hit it out from within one yard of the nearest corner, no player of the attacking side at that time shall be within 20 yards of the goal line, and the defenders, with the exception of the goal-keeper, must be behind their goal line.

5.—When the ball goes off at the side, a player of the opposite side to that which hit it out shall roll it out from the point on the boundary line at which it went off at right angles with the boundary line, and it shall not be in play until it has touched the ice, and the 'player rolling it in shall not play it until it has been played by another player, every player being then behind the ball.

6.—On the infringement of any of the above rules, the ball shall be brought back and a Bully shall take place.

7.—All disputes shall be settled by the Umpires, or in the event of their disagreement, by the Referee.

The rules of hockey as first published in The Gazette of Montreal, Feb. 27, 1877. Only one word, "ice" for "ball" differed from the field hockey rules created in England in 1875. The printed set of playing rules is recorded in a scrapbook recorded by the Montreal Amateur Athletic Association.   *PAC C837 87*

APPENDIX B
Laws of Hockey—Canada—1905

Dartmouth Hockey League

Schedule, 1905.

PRINTED AT PATRIOT OFFICE.

19

LAWS OF HOCKEY.

Sec. 1. A team shall be composed of seven players who shall be bona fide members of the Clubs they represent. No player shall be allowed to play on more than one team in the same series during a season.

Sec. 2. The game shall be commenced and renewed by a face in the centre of the rink. Goals shall be six feet wide and four feet high, and provided with goal nets, such as approved of by the League.

DEFINITION OF A FACE.

The puck shall be faced by being dropped between the sticks of two opponents, and the referee then calling "play."

The goals shall be placed at least five feet from the edge of the ice.

Sec. 3. Two half-hours, with an intermission of ten minutes between will be the time allowed for matches, but no stops of more than fifteen minutes will be allowed. A match will be decided by the team winning the greatest number of games during that time. In case of a tie after playing the specified two-half hours, play will continue until one side secures a game, unless otherwise

21

agreed upon between the captains before the match. Goals shall be changed after each half-hour.

Sec. 4. No change of players shall be made after a match has commenced, except for reasons of accidents or injury during the game.

Sec. 5. Should any player be injured during the first half of the match and compelled to leave the ice, his side shall be allowed to put on a spare man from the reserve to equalize the teams; should any player be injured during the second half of the match the captain of the opposing team shall have the option of dropping a player to equalize the teams or allow his opponents to put on a man from the reserve. In the event of any dispute between the captains as to the injured players fitness to continue the game, the matter shall at once be decided by the referee.

Sec. 6. Should the game be temporarily stopped by the infringement of any of the rules, the captain of the opposing team may claim that the puck be taken back and a face take place where it was last played from before such infringement occurred.

Sec. 7. When a player hits the puck, anyone of the same side who at such moment of hitting is

23

nearer the opponent's goal line is out of play, and may not touch the puck himself or in any way whatever prevent any other player from doing so, until the puck has been played. A player should always be on his own side of the puck.

Sec. 8. The puck may be stopped, but not carried or knocked on by any part of the body, nor shall any player close his hand on or carry the puck to the ice in his hand. No player shall raise his stick above the shoulder, except in lifting the puck. Charging from behind, tripping, collaring, kicking, or checking another player who has not possession of the puck, or shinning shall not be allowed, and for any infringement of these rules the referee may rule the offending player off the ice for that match, or for such portion of actual playing time as he may see fit.

Sec. 9. When the puck goes off the ice or a foul occurs behind the goals it shall be taken by the referee to five yards at right angles from the goal line and there faced. When the puck goes off the ice at the sides it shall be taken by the referee to five yards at right angles from the boundary line and there faced.

Sec. 10. The goal keeper must not during play lie, kneel or sit upon the ice, but must maintain a standing position.

Sec. 11. Goal shall be scored when the puck

24

shall have passed between the goal posts from in front below an imaginary line across the top of posts.

Sec. 12. Hockey sticks shall not be more than three inches wide at any part.

Sec. 13. The puck must be made of vulcanized rubber, one inch thick all through and three inches in diameter.

Sec. 14. The captains of the contesting teams shall agree upon a referee and two umpires (one to be stationed behind each goal) which positions shall not be changed during a match, and two time-keepers. In the event of the captains failing to agree on umpires and time-keepers the referee shall appoint same.

Sec. 15. All disputes during the match shall be decided by the referee, and he shall have full control of all players and officials from commencement to finish of matches, inclusive of stops, and his decision shall be final.

Sec. 16. All questions as to games shall be settled by the umpires, and their decision shall be final.

Sec. 17. In the event of any dispute as to the decision of an umpire or time-keeper the referee shall have power to remove and replace him.

Sec. 18. Any player guilty of using profane or abusive language to any officials or other players shall be liable to be ruled off by the referee, as per section 8.

Sec. 19. The referee shall report to the Executive-Committee any player for persistent infringement of the rules. The committee to have power to deal with the case as they see fit.

APPENDIX C

BUILD YOUR OWN HOCKEY RINK

WHEN zero comes and ground is hard,
We take the hose and flood the yard;
I like the garden, but I think
I like it better as a rink.

Since I was eight or nine years old, I have had a fascination with building a hockey rink in my backyard. In fact, at about age ten, I suffered the ultimate hockey injury on my homemade rink—the loss of half of my front tooth, which, coincidentally, was repaired by my first hockey coach, Dr. Graham Conrad.

I resumed my rink construction efforts about ten years ago to give my children a place to learn to skate. Although most people think that our climate is too mild for a successful ice surface, this has not been my experience. During the last decade, I have usually had ice from Christmas week to early March. The secret for

success is to create a rink that can survive the periodic thaws that we inevitably receive during the winter months. The following is a summary of the system that I have used.

The Yard

The most important ingredient for a successful back yard rink is obviously a relatively flat and fairly large back yard. A simple procedure that I have used to survey the "back forty" involves a string, two sticks or large spikes, and a level. Choosing the highest point of the yard, I attach the string to the head of the spike and push it into the ground so the string is at ground level. Walking across the yard the approximate dimension of the rink, I hammer the other spike slightly into the ground and adjust the string until it is level. (If the centre of your yard is the highest point, start from there and check the slope in all directions.) The length of the spike

Slope of yard

above the ground gives you an approximate height of the change in slope on the ground. I always try to have a minimum of 2 inches (5cm) of ice. If the string on the spike or stick is 6 inches (15 cm) above the ground, the side of the rink on the low end will have to be about 8 inches (20 cm). Don't despair if your yard has a big slope; my friend, Dr. Graham Conrad Jr., uses about three feet of railway ties on one side of his rink in Amherst. Before proceeding with the actual construction, it is important to define the four corners of the rink on the ground. I build a rink that is approximately 30' x 50' (10m x 16m).

The Frame

When building the rink, I basically create a large wading pool in the yard. This is accomplished by building a wooden frame around the perimeter of the rink and filling it in with plastic. The frame construction is usually done with boards that range in size from 2 x 6 inches to 2 x 10 inches. I screw these together using braces on the outside surface of the boards. At the corners, I let the boards overlap to give the structure extra strength.

The Tarp and Plastic

After the frame has been built, I cover the rink with a large tarp. These are available in various sizes; use a white one if possible because they absorb less heat

from the sun. Make certain that the tarp extends over the top of the frame to allow for bracing.

The tarp serves two purposes—it protects the thinner plastic layer from sticks or rocks that might puncture the plastic, and it provides a second layer of protection in the event there is a hole in the final plastic layer. The plastic, which is normally in the range of 6 mm thick, is placed on top of the tarp so that it covers the entire rink surface. I normally purchase a roll of plastic that is 50 x 100 feet, which provides enough plastic for two winters. Although you can attempt to use one piece two years in a row, this increases the chance of holes in the plastic, which can be detrimental to the success of the project.

It is important to choose the proper time for the installation of the tarp and plastic. They both form a large kite if there is any wind which makes installation very difficult. I have found that the hour or two before sunset is the time of day with the least amount of wind. My wife, Ann, and I are usually able to install the wood, tarp, and plastic in about three hours—it usually takes us another three hours to reconcile afterwards!

Water and Ice

As soon as the plastic is installed, start to fill the rink with the garden house. This can take many hours and it is important to get the plastic covered with water as quickly as possible before the wind increases. I like to fill the water to the desired depth as soon as possible. The water can sit for days until the temperature is cold enough for it to freeze. Once I have the top coat of ice, I can relax and wait for the entire rink to turn to a solid block. This normally only takes one or two days. After the ice is formed, changes in weather are irrelevant— the ice may melt but it will re-freeze without any loss of water. The final step after the ice is

solid is to add the crest of your favourite team to centre ice. I found laminated place mats with team crests for a couple of dollars which can be covered with a layer of ice.

The rink will require periodic re-surfacing—just sweep off the snow and cover the ice with a centimetre of water and soon the rink's surface will be as smooth as glass. (Make certain that you drain the garden hose completely to avoid the water freezing inside the hose!) The last few years have seen the installation of a halogen light, which provides perfect lighting conditions during the long evenings.

One final point—make certain you wear a helmet and face mask. Take it from me, it is no fun losing a tooth on the rink! The good news is that you and your family will have hours of fun and actually look forward to cold winter days and nights. My children often skate at lunch hour during school days. On a beautiful, clear winter's evening, don't forget to lie on your back on the ice and look up at the

many stars in the night sky. When the children are in bed, you might even sneak out for a romantic skate in the moonlight!

The winter of 2002 was the worst I have experienced for rink building. I was pleased to see that Halifax Regional Municipality was assisting with the construction of outdoor rinks. As well, don't worry about the grass—I have never had a problem after removing the plastic when the ice melts. Have fun and happy skating!

A HOCKEY TRIP TO MONTREAL

It is somewhat ironic that I grew up in Dartmouth a lifetime fan of the Montreal Canadiens. I'll never forget our family pilgrimage to hockey's shrine—the Montreal Forum—in 1970. It was the March school break and my father, David, decided to take my grandfather, brother, and me on the traditional Maritime right of passage into boyhood—a trip by train to Montreal to watch our beloved Canadiens. What a week! The hockey game was fantastic—Montreal defeated New York and I was thrilled. My father wasn't as impressed—I got lost and he spent an entire period looking for me as I watched the game from the aisle behind the Habs' bench. Poor Serge Savard broke his leg (I returned to Montreal for a second game in the seventies and he broke it again). After the game, we met true professionals like Jean Beliveau and Robert Rousseau, who insisted on staying behind to sign autographs for star-struck ten year olds.

Our excitement continued throughout the week. After an impromptu visit to Mayor Jean Drapeau at City Hall, we met golfer George Knudson at Simpson's and received a bag of plastic golf tees. I caught my shoe in an escalator in the train station and caused a major traffic jam as hundreds of commuters vaulted over me. We watched the St. Patrick's Day parade, which seemed most peculiar to a young boy—everything green in a French-speaking city in a snowstorm.

Hockey Heaven, The Forum

JEAN BELIVEAU   CENTER
MONTREAL CANADIENS

Record Your Own Hockey History

Player's Name: _____

Favourite hockey team: _____

Favourite player: _____

Favourite old timer: _____

Year: _____

Team played: _____

Position: _____

Coaches: _____

Sweater Number: _____

Goals: _____

Assists: _____

Team Friends and Positions: _____

Most Memorable Hockey Trip: _____

Player's Name: _____

Favourite hockey team: _____

Favourite player: _____

Favourite old timer: _____

Year: _____

Team played: _____

Position: _____

Coaches: _____

Sweater Number: _____

Goals: _____

Assists: _____

Team Friends and Positions: _____

Most Memorable Hockey Trip: _____

IMAGE SOURCES

Black Cultural Centre: 96

Caldwell, Tom: 24

A Canadian Child's ABC (1931): 112

Canoe '97: 16; 102

Dartmouth Heritage Museum: title page (photo by T. Osawa); vii (photo by T. Osawa); 6; 15; 18; 22; 28; 29 (photo by M. Jones); 31; 32; 37 (photo by T. Osawa); 46 (photo by M. Jones); 50 (photo by T. Osawa); 51 (photo by T. Osawa); 53 (photo by T. Osawa); 55; 56; 57 (top, photo by M. Jones); 59; 60 (bottom, photo by M. Jones); 66 (right, photo by T. Osawa); 67 (photo by T. Osawa); 68 (photo by T. Osawa); 69; 71; 73 (photo by T. Osawa); 81; 84; 93 (top, photo by T. Osawa); 101 (top, photo by M. Jones); 108-111

Fitsell, Bill: 107

Forrestall, Tom: 41

Heritage Trust of Nova Scotia, *A Century Ago Halifax 1871* (1970): 56; 58

HRM: 71 (bottom); 72

Jones, David: 3; 4 (bottom); 116 (left)

Jones, Martin: 2 (Scotia Bank); 4 (top); 5 (Gene Mattatal); 19; 34; 42; 44 (bottom); 52; 57; 60 (top); 61; 63; 64; 70; 79; 83; 90 (bottom); 98 (D. & D. Krochko; 100; 101 (bottom); 116 (Opeechee); 112-115; 117

MacLeod, John: 76

Martin, Gerald: 95

Nova Scotia Archives and Records Management: 11; 14; 17; 23; 25; 26; 33; 39; 44 (top); 57 (bottom, photo by M. Jones); 62; 75; 77; 85; 89; 90 (top); 92; 94; 97.

Nova Scotia Sport Hall of Fame: cover (photo by M. Jones); 20 (photos by M. Jones); 66 (left); 82; 93 (bottom)

Rogers, Anna Ruth: 84 (top)

Underwriters' Survey Bureau Limited: 27